C000243532

Getting it Right in Reception

Getting it Right in Reception

Neil Farmer

BLOOMSBURY

LONDON · OXFORD · NEW YORK · NEW DELHI · SYDNEY

Featherstone Education

An imprint of Bloomsbury Publishing Plc

50 Bedford Square
London
WC1B 3DP
UK

1385 Broadway
New York
NY 10018
USA

www.bloomsbury.com

Featherstone Education is a registered trademark of Bloomsbury Publishing Plc

First published 2016

British Library Cataloguing-in-Publication Data
A catalogue record for this book is available from the British Library.

ISBN: PB: 978-1-4729-3071-2
      ePub: 978-1-4729-3073-6
      ePDF: 978-1-4729-3072-9

Library of Congress Cataloging-in-Publication Data
A catalog record for this book is available from the Library of Congress.

10 9 8 7 6 5 4 3 2 1

Typeset by Newgen Knowledge Works (P) Ltd., Chennai, India
Printed and bound in India by Replika Pvt. Ltd.

This book is produced using paper that is made from wood grown in managed, sustainable forests.
It is natural, renewable and recyclable. The logging and manufacturing processes conform to the
environmental regulations of the country of origin.

To view more of our titles please visit **www.bloomsbury.com**

Contents

Acknowledgements vii

Introduction 1
A look at the Reception year 1
Changes in the Foundation Stage 5
Transition into Reception 7
A quick word on leadership 10
Using this book 11

**Chapter 1: The revised common inspection framework and
              everyday practice 15**
Getting to grips with the expectations 15
A look at the common inspection framework 17
British values 22
School readiness 24

Chapter 2: Getting the basics right 31
Developing an overall strategic vision for your Reception class 31
From vision to practice 41
Growth mindsets 41
What is behaviour for learning? 43

Chapter 3: Routines and environment 47
Developing a routine 48
Developing learning environments that are fit for purpose 55

Chapter 4: Observation, assessment and planning 63
Observing to inform planning 63
What is observation? 65
Learning detectives 68
Planning 72

Chapter 5: Discrete challenges and shared success criteria 81
Discrete challenges 82
Shared success criteria 87

Chapter 6: Progress 91

What constitutes typical progress? 92
Transition into Year 1 and life without levels 97
Development of language 97
How aspirational are you for your children? 99

Chapter 7: Leading an effective Reception class team 105

How to recruit the right people for your team 106
What will you need to successfully grow, develop and lead your team? 107
What makes a good Reception year leader? 109
Monitoring your impact as a leader 111
Leadership and monitoring quality 114

Conclusion 123

Appendices 125

Appendix 1: Sample aspiration, skills and development map across the
    Foundation Stage 125
Appendix 2: End of year data analysis 129
Appendix 3: Progression of successful text reading through EYFS, KS1 and KS2 134
Appendix 4: Example action plan 135
Bibliography and further reading 139

Acknowledgements

I would like to thank a number of people who have greatly supported and assisted me in the writing of this book: Helen Diamond at Bloomsbury who so kindly accepted my initial proposal and assisted greatly in organising my thoughts; Emily Wilson, my editor, relentless in the pursuit of getting it right on the page and for keeping me on track as I do tend to wander sometimes; the many headteachers and practitioners who have entrusted me to support and develop their Reception practice; and finally, my wonderful wife Margaret, who has patiently listened to my thoughts, moans and frustration and kept me going when a glass of wine might be beckoning.

Special thanks go to the following schools for allowing me to include photographs and documents in this publication.

Hale School, Farnham

Hamsey Green Primary School, Warlingham

Iqra Primary School, Slough

Kingfisher Community Primary School, Chatham

Manorfield Primary and Nursery School, Horley

Salfords Primary School, Redhill

Send C of E First School, Woking

St. James C of E Primary School, Weybridge

St Mary's Catholic Infant School, Croydon

The Grange Community Infant School, Addlestone

Winterbourne Nursery and Infant School, Croydon

I am also indebted to the wonderful children, staff and leadership at the following schools, with whom I have worked, supported, cajoled and indeed learnt a great deal from.

Chivenor Primary School, Birmingham

Cranleigh Infant School, Cranleigh

Downsview Primary School, Croydon

George Eliot Primary School, St. John's Wood

Godolphin Infant School, Slough

Lakeside Primary School, Camberley

Littleton Church of England Infant School, Shepperton

Lordswood School, Chatham

Moss Lane School, Godalming

Oakington Manor Primary School, Wembley

Park Mead Primary, Cranleigh

Park Lane Primary School, Nuneaton

Perry Wood Primary and Nursery School, Worcester
Prior Heath Infant School, Camberley
Redriff Primary School, Southwark
Riverley Primary School, Leyton
Saxon Way Primary School, Gillingham
Smitham Primary School, Coulsdon
St Peter's C of E Primary School, Farnham
St Thomas Becket Catholic Primary School, Croydon
Surrey Hills C of E Primary School, Dorking
Warren Mead Infant School, Banstead
Wayfield Primary School, Chatham
Willow Brook Primary School Academy, Leyton
Woodmansterne Primary School, Lambeth

Introduction

'Reception' – it's a funny old term: a waiting room, a foyer, or a gathering place before the main event. The main event here being the start of Key Stage 1, and supposed school life proper. Consequently, Reception has to a greater extent been seen as a 'holding pen', a preparation for 'school readiness' rather than a stage and age in its own right.

I have been privileged in my working life to work with the youngest of primary school children. Their natural desire to learn, to explore, to question, to bounce back and find things out is infectious. I have also been fortunate to work with a large number of schools and dedicated professionals across the country and abroad. Although they were at different stages in their development, they all aimed to be the best they could possibly be and to afford the children the best start to not only their school life but life in general.

In my many guises I have worked as a class teacher, phase leader and school leader. I have supported private, voluntary and independent (PVI) settings during my time as an advisory teacher and a cross section of primary schools in my role as Foundation Stage consultant. I have been the strategic lead for early years in a number of authorities, overseeing the development of the workforce and putting in place systems and strategies that resulted in improved outcomes for children, a narrowing of the gap and improved Ofsted outcomes across all the sectors. I have also been a school improvement adviser to numerous schools and now work independently supporting whole school developments. My heart and passion, however, lies in the Foundation Stage – which to me runs to at least seven years of age – working in co-operation with school leaders, governors, and Foundation Stage practitioners, re-evaluating practice and provision and overseeing the strategic direction of learning and teaching and delivering high-quality outcomes for the children and the school.

A look at the Reception year

Through my travels up and down the country and on flights to far-flung places, I have often pondered about Reception classes and the practitioners who work in them. What do these practitioners have in place to support them and give them guidance – a framework, or skeleton, of proven strategies on which to build upon and give them confidence to state, 'This is what we are doing and why'. The results will speak for themselves.

There are numerous publications on and about 'the early years', some deeply theoretical, some looking at particular strands or areas of learning and many others focusing primarily on the age ranges just below that of Reception children – so there is a void. This book intends, in part, to fill some of that void and empower Reception practitioners, and here I mean all those working in the Reception classes, to make decisions and put in place agreed and shared principles, routines, systems and physical and emotional environments which meet the needs of four- and five-year-olds – underpinned by a firm pedagogic approach, high aspirations and expectations which remain constant.

'How' the learning and teaching is carried out remains constant and is embedded and shared by all – rigorously monitored and evaluated by leadership so it becomes irrelevant 'who' is delivering it as all stakeholders share the same passion and understanding of how young children acquire knowledge and develop in your school.

'What' the children learn at different times and the skills they develop is a movable feast depending on the children's interests and stages of development.

Yes, I will be delving into the realms of theory and research, but I will be putting it in its proper place, which is in the classroom, and looking at the impact it has on young learners and practitioners alike.

> *I suppose I am like a cherry picker, and that is what practitioners should be. Reading research, arguing with it, implementing some of it, blending it with other research and theoretical approaches and coming up with something personal – rather like a good Bordeaux – complex, subtle, strong, unique, but immensely satisfying and getting better with age and experience.*

It is important to remember that the Reception year is part of the Foundation Stage, a unique stage of development with its own curriculum, its own outcomes and its own pedagogic approach. Good schools are now taking this approach forward into Key Stage 1 and beyond as they look to develop the skills and attributes young children have acquired through this responsible pedagogic approach and build upon the 'Characteristics of Effective Learning' (see page 9) and the positive attitudes towards learning fostered in the Foundation Stage.

Later in the book I will draw reference to a number of schools I have supported in developing this approach in Key Stage 1. The involvement of the children in their learning in these schools is testament to this revised approach. Children are given time to practise new skills and knowledge and embed learning. Routines have been revised, outdoor environments developed and there is a greater emphasis on independent learning, self-review, autonomy and challenge. Results and progress in these schools is phenomenal. These are what I would term 'great schools' – they have an intangible feeling in the air: one of purpose, industry, learning and collaboration shared between all stakeholders.

In this book I am not ignoring the fantastic work that many nurseries do. In fact, this book aims to build upon that emergent work, and I will delve deeper into this later in this section when transition is discussed (page 7).

Many Reception practitioners feel isolated, especially those who work in a single form entry school with no nursery, and where the pressure to change their practice into a more formal approach that is more akin to a primary school can be almost overwhelming. I often find that schools at risk of falling into a 'Requires Improvement' Ofsted category or finding themselves already in one, adopt practices that are at odds with the requirements of the Early Years Foundation Stage (EYFS). It is in these schools that the children are most vulnerable, and adults feel under the most pressure. There have been many times when I have heard practitioners in these settings say, 'We need to add more formality to the Reception classes to get them ready'.

Ready for what I argue? Sitting at tables, being compliant, being reliant on adults and being told what to do – is this good learning or behaviour for learning? I find this methodology puzzling and too short term in approach, and that I think is the key issue. Schools are under increasing pressure to deliver results that are tangible and measurable, but is this approach preparing children for an independent and fulfilling life once they have left the relative safety of the school gates? We are currently preparing children for a life in the future that we have no understanding or comprehension of. What will the job market, life–work balance and emotional security be like? All of this we do not know. What we do know is that tomorrow's adults will need a set of personal qualities quite different from those of yesteryear. These will undoubtedly include:

- persistence
- resilience
- courage
- positive self-image and self-esteem
- co-operation.

The key question is, how are schools doing this, when the focus might be on short-term gains in SATs, grammar and phonics test results and the maddening assumption that all children should be progressing at similar rates through the year groups?

Somewhere along the way it has been forgotten, or ignored, that humans are unique beings who learn at different rates and in different ways and different things at different times.

Quick gains are not often truly embedded in the soul; they are rapidly forgotten as they are not regularly practised – otherwise we would be expecting all babies to be walking at a year and speaking articulately at two years of age. We know that this is nonsense. What children, and I would argue also adults need, is time to practise skills and knowledge and apply them in meaningful contexts to be able to internalise them and have shared ownership of the learning and assessment.

I firmly believe that the greatest Foundation Stage practitioners have total empathy with the children in their charge. They innately see the world from the perspective and viewpoint of the children, and they involve them wholeheartedly in the development of the whole learning environment. In my experience, it is the Foundation Stage practitioners who are the best company at the staff meal or evening out – they view education in a different light; they understand the requirements of the child before the requirements of the curriculum and see that developing a child's aspirations and desire to learn is as important, if not more so, than what they learn and when. Always think how you do things best, what are your requirements, how you might need some 'down time' after a busy period at work and put this into practice with your children – you will feel inordinately better for it, and far more confident in your approach to learning and teaching. The key question to ask yourself every day in your classroom is: 'What is it like for a child here?'

This reminds me of a visit I made to a school where, by her own admission, the headteacher had little understanding of the Foundation Stage and saw it, in the main, as 'lots of playing about and no learning'. We were walking over to the Reception classes and spied three boys highly engaged in some sort of play that involved the use of long rectangular blocks. 'See,' said the headteacher with a disapproving look, 'playing about'. I urged her not to be too hasty and judgmental with her initial observation and suggested listening in to uncover the true extent of what was taking place – hoping beyond hope that there was indeed some purpose and learning going on, as I had been supporting the Reception classes.

It transpired that the boys were engaged in a game – Star Wars – and the long rectangular blocks were the lightsabers. On closer scrutiny we also discovered that the boys had drawn a square at the rear of the storage shed, and using their emergent phonics had scrawled 'saftee zon' in bright yellow chalk on the ground. Talking with the boys, we were proudly informed that this 'saftee zon' was where the batteries of the lightsabres could be recharged, and more importantly, you couldn't 'get dead' in it. The adults in the Reception class had condoned the 'game' and urged the boys to come up with other options and areas to play in, alluding to roles and responsibilities in the play – use of imagination, language development, co-operation and negotiation were all in evidence. The game was extended by the adults who intervened when and where necessary to set our intrepid trio with new challenges and adventures.

I remarked to the headteacher that perhaps the sole reason that the boys came to school that day was to play their game under the responsible stewardship of the sensitive and stimulating adults – not to do phonics, literacy, numeracy or any other area of learning, but to play, to be, to do and unwittingly to learn. I think that this is an important issue to remember. What is the hook that gets the children into school and genuinely excites them? You know as adults, that if something doesn't meet your needs or requirements the chances of you going back a second time are pretty slim. The children in our Reception classes do not have that option. They have to go, this is not negotiable, and so let us give them the environment, the skills, the time and space, and the excitement they desperately need.

I often remark to Reception practitioners that a good Reception class should be like a favourite shop – lots of new interesting, fascinating things, a good line of solid staples and, as any excellent retailer does, a positive response to the clientele.

A two-tiered approach is crucial – raising standards are part of that approach, but the key question is how do we achieve the high standards required alongside a set of core principles that put the children at the centre of learning and equip them with a skill set that will last them throughout their lives? What is this 'otherness' that great schools have in abundance? This is something that I will be exploring throughout the course of this book.

The term 'Foundation Stage' is crucial. Early years practitioners are putting in place the foundations for future learning capacity. Rather like the foundations of a building – get these footings right with the correct mixture, and the ensuing structure will last a lifetime. Evidence suggests that good early years results can protect children's emotional well-being and self-esteem through a poor primary phase and into secondary school. The key purpose of the Foundation Stage is to equip our young children with the tools and dispositions to carry on learning, to see themselves as capable and confident, to be resilient, to accept challenge and set back and have the fortitude to carry on, or, as I usually say, to 'Crack on!'.

Changes in the Foundation Stage

Changes are afoot in the Foundation Stage. Base line assessment at four years of age will be taking place within the next two years. From September 2016, the only recognised starting point will be an approved baseline assessment; this baseline will sit within teachers' broader assessments of children's learning. As of September 2016, the EYFS profile will no longer be compulsory, although I would suggest that schools continue to use the documentation in terms of final attainment which will ease the transition into Year 1. The progress children make from the Reception class to Year 6 will be seen as just as important as their final attainment. The EYFS will, however, continue to be statutory, supporting children in experiencing a broad and engaging programme of learning in Reception.

It all seems quite complicated, but the thing is not to panic. Don't drop your elements of great practice in the face of new legislation. In fact, great early years practice has not altered at all over the ages. All it requires is patience, genuineness, understanding, open-ended resources and an innate understanding of how young children learn. It is not, and never has been, about certain resources, intervention schemes or governmental interference. It is not about focused teaching, but rather the moment by moment interactions adults have with young children to coach, mediate and support them. This 'moment by moment' teaching is the cornerstone to outstanding early years practice and teaching overall, and is often overlooked by outsiders who prefer to see a more rigid, focused approach in operation.

Think of yourself as a parent – do you have focused teaching sessions at home? Probably not! Shared reading and writing will happen every day, but the majority of the quality interactions and learning will come through the 'moment by moment' stuff that you do every day without even thinking about it. In the classroom, you need to ensure that you have robust systems in place that will allow you to do this and demonstrate that all children make realistic yet rapid progress in the Reception class relative to their starting points.

The hungry brain

In her article, 'A hungry brain slurps up a kid's energy', Laura Sanders discusses some key research findings about brain development in young children by Christopher Kuzawa and his team, published in the **Proceedings of the National Academy of Sciences**:

'A child's body remains small for so long because the brain hogs all the energy. A 5-year-old's brain actually burns more glucose than an adult's … Around age 4, the brain accounts for a whopping 43 percent of the body's total energy expenditure, the team estimates, a massive allotment that might divert resources from a growing body. Interestingly, this age might also be around the time children physically slow down a little bit. Activity levels of preschoolers seem to be a bit lower than those of older children, earlier studies have suggested. The body might be taking a rest and instead sending its resources to the energy-hogging brain.'

It is important that Reception practitioners are aware of this and have routines, expectations and environments that support and nurture this natural phenomenon and give the brain the food, the excitement and rest it needs to develop and learn. The key things here to remember and to take into consideration are your routines and your environments. Do you provide nourishing and energy-supplying snacks for children so they can recharge this energy-munching machine in their heads and keep the learning processes going? Learning, taking in, assimilating and practising new knowledge is exhausting for young children and I do not think that there is enough thought put into school routines to ensure that the expended energy is sufficiently replaced or that the rhythms and routines of the day mirror the times when children are most mentally active.

Question for reflection

- Are the children in your Reception class living their dreams?

Transition into Reception

For children in many schools the beginning of the Reception year is the start of their school career – not all schools are fortunate enough to have a nursery attached and therefore the physical move to a new setting full of unfamiliar people, sights and smells can be profoundly unsettling.

The *Kirklees guidance for transitions in The Early Years* (2013) poses five key questions:

1 'Is the impact of a positive transition experience acknowledged with the school/ setting?

2 Is transition given priority at appropriate times of the year?

3 Is there ongoing communication between providers through the year?

4 Do governors, committee members, managers and headteachers give transition the time it needs?

5 Are the contributions from every provider and parent valued?'

It is vital that there is a flow of information between the school and any feeder setting. The EYFS Framework clearly states that information on children's personal and academic progress should be shared between all stakeholders, and this includes parents before and during the transition process.

'Transition should be seen as a process, not an event, and should be planned for and discussed with children and parents. Settings should communicate information which will secure continuity of experience for the child between settings.' (Department for children, schools and families, *Practice Guidance for the Early Years Foundation Stage* 2008)

Transition is a term or concept that I do not necessarily believe in. Schools seem to put a time frame on transition: 'Oh yes, we do transition up until half-term'. What does that mean exactly? Does that mean that we accept what went on beforehand for a short time and then put it to bed and start something new? Synonyms of 'transition' include: changeover, passing and conversion. Is this what we are doing from year to year – saying, 'Thanks for that! Now it's time for a changeover.'? Transition is 'a process not an event', it is a never-ending cycle of review and movement, building upon what went before and adding to it. If you look at transition in the long term, it does not represent a problem. If the nursery routines and expectations will be different in September than they are by the following

July, this is the same in Reception – things alter as the children progress and grow. Thus routines and environments at the start of the Reception year should mirror those at the end of the time in nursery – as the children then grow, expectations within their known environment will change. Children will have access to the same resources, but the key questions to ask are: what is different and what are the increased expectations – otherwise the children will merely be repeating the nursery year.

In the not too distant past, it could take at least half a term before all the children were attending the Reception class full-time. 'On entry' was a long drawn out process that became somewhat of a saga for schools. Looking back, this was justified as 'settling the children in, getting to know them, etc.' This is no longer acceptable as it wastes valuable learning time. Although not all schools have an attached nursery, the majority of children will be entering Reception having had an experience of either a nursery or pre-school, some for prolonged hours of the day – they are already pretty resilient little creatures with a multitude of experiences and have already worked out emergent strategies with which to cope. Often it is the parents who see this step into Reception as a massive leap – it is not, it is the natural order of things.

Many nurseries produce wonderful 'learning journeys' of the children's time with them – highlighting and celebrating achievements with photos and samples of 'work'. These should be part of the transition process. In reality, however, the Reception class teacher cannot store them all, for often they might be in different formats (e.g. files, scrapbooks etc.) It is best practice, if possible, to take some of this evidence as the starting point of the learning journey in Reception. If the nursery is part of the school this is far easier as the formats should be the same so continuity is already in place – or at least it should be.

Ideally the Reception practitioners meet all the children before they start in Reception – either in nursery or on the school site – but it is often difficult to organise this, especially if the children come from a multitude of settings, and likewise for the nurseries if their children are moving on to numerous schools. Obviously schools hold open days at the end of the summer term for the nursery children and this, by and large, works well as it gives the new staff the opportunity to meet the children and families.

Often the only information the Reception classes might receive is the 'learning journey' and the tracking of progress through the nursery – and herein lies a problem in itself. Too often there is a lack of understanding of child development in many settings and accordingly the 'data' can show that many children – and a high proportion of new entrants to Reception – have already achieved the Early Learning Goals. Conversely, I have also been given data showing children leaving nursery apparently still operating within the 22–36 month band, where the question must be raised: 'What have you being doing?' This is a real issue for schools with no attached nursery, and one which requires urgent intervention on behalf of local authorities in the training provided on child development, so that the nurseries are able to complete a comprehensive picture of development and the receiving schools are able to give the children developmentally what it is they require.

Conversations with feeder settings are vital, often not necessarily to gain information on levels of development but rather on the 'Characteristics of effective teaching and learning'

– how the children are, their experiences in the broader sense, what they like, what are their interests, how they tackle situations and relate, initially, to unfamiliar adults.

Characteristics of effective teaching and learning

The three characteristics of effective teaching and learning, as described in the *Statutory framework for the early years foundation stage*, are:

1 'Playing and exploring – children investigate and experience things, and "have a go"

2 Active learning – children concentrate and keep on trying if they encounter difficulties, and enjoy achievements

3 Creating and thinking critically – children have and develop their own ideas, make links between ideas, and develop strategies for doing things.'

The question of home visits and whether parents/carers should be allowed in the classroom

In short, the answer should be a resounding 'yes' to both of these questions. If we start with the latter, in too many schools the parental link is not strengthened, and indeed often weakened, by a no admission policy into the classroom. This is often excused under the guise of 'children gaining independence'. But let's look at this realistically. The oldest child in the classoom is five-years-old and the youngest has only just turned four-years-old. There is often an unseemly desire to develop children at a faster rate than is absolutely necessary. We are only four and five once in our lives so let's allow the children the opportunity to enjoy it and put in the required support around them. Added to this is the requirement of the EYFS that states the need to foster positive relationships with parents as they are the primary carers of the children and often have in-depth knowledge and understanding of their child's personality and needs. To shut them out in the playground, to me, is plainly ridiculous and takes away one strut of the supportive triangle.

For many parents, the start of Reception is the step into 'big school' and quite often there are unrealistic expectations attached to this. It is the job and responsibility of Reception teachers to allay these expectations, explain how the children will be learning and the realistic expectations of them – this can only be done if there is a transparent, open and respectful relationship between all parties.

In many cases there is a reluctance on the part of the parents to enter the school building. This may be due to an unfortunate and unhappy experience that they might have encountered or experienced. The old limbic system kicks in – the smells, the sights and the sounds of the school flood back and there is a definite switch off in the brain that says, 'Urghh! I remember this'. Our job is to get parents in, make them feel welcome, ensure the environment is pleasing to all the senses and share with them how their children will be learning in the fascinating world of the Reception class. I cannot understand the mentality that keeps parents out of the school – they are our primary clients and we need to be showcasing what the school does well. Also, how can we really expect parents to interact and support the school if we lock them out from the start?

Some schools prefer to involve parents first thing in the morning during 'early work' sessions when the parents can support and work alongside their children. It is important to make it clear that this is about the learning and not about the parents doing things for their children. At St Marys' in Croydon, this 'early bird work' is rotational with groups who are set different challenges that are pitched at the correct level of competency. In other establishments this process is more open – both approaches are highly successful in engaging the parents in the learning process. Conversely, in other establishments there have been issues in getting reluctant parents through the door in the morning – there's always the excuse of a hospital appointment, awaiting a delivery or something similar. To counter this, Godolphin Infants in Slough would open the doors at the end of the session fifteen minutes early each day – the thinking behind this being that parents had to pick their children up, so would come into the class at the end of the day and join in the learning plenaries, number games, phonic input etc. to find out how their children are learning. This methodology has had positive outcomes in terms of parental support in learning and a greater sense of community.

Home visits for Reception are something that often splits opinion – I would argue that they should take place because a percentage of children will have no experience of pre-school or nursery and many will be below the statutory school age – why wouldn't we visit them in the place that they may feel most secure and with the people who know them best? Such a policy would obviously have ramifications on logistics; some schools offer home visits to children who did not attend the school nursery, others to all children – this is a decision that will need to be made. It is all about building that relationship between the home and the school and valuing the home as an equal partner in the learning process.

The key question is when to undertake them. I would argue to do this as early as possible, but schools often undertake any visits at the end of the summer term, when the transition processes are in full swing and there may be greater flexibility – again these are decisions to be made.

A quick word on leadership

The theme of leadership will run throughout the book, looking in particular at the aspects of leadership required in the differing contexts of the chapters. Leadership is the crucial element in any field. Structures require strong and consistent leadership if they are going to maintain greatness, reflect and improve further. Leaders drive through improvements and are solid in their vision and purpose, they motivate others and through engagement realign ways of thinking. Leaders identify strengths within systems and people and put in place structures that support the overall vision and the individuals within it.

Being a leader is not an easy option. A leader must be a radiator – one who radiates vitality and strength of purpose – not a drain, who virtually sucks the life out of people. A leader must be adaptable but have a core set of principles that underpin their practice and gives them and their team the confidence to say, 'This is what we do, this is why and these are the results'.

Using this book

The aim of this book is to give Reception teachers and leaders some clear, concise and practical advice and suggested guidance for how to develop and build upon their practice – so they become more confident in their pedagogical approach and in their ability to deliver a purposeful and meaningful curriculum which meets the needs of all their children, and allows them to fully develop as confident, capable learners. All the strategies discussed in the book have been highly successful in raising outcomes for children, empowering Reception teachers and leaders, and in ensuring that the Reception year is a magical experience for the children.

The book is divided into seven chapters, starting with the core basics of enshrining an agreed pedagogic approach to learning and teaching and then moving through the practical arrangements of the environments, planning and assessment, and concluding with practical guidance on recording children's progress and monitoring the quality of the Reception class. Readers are invited to use the chapters in isolation, dependent on where they are on the journey of development, or use as a complete whole for putting in place coherent and workable structures.

I have structured the book in what could be construed as chronological order and all chapters are inter-related and impinge on each other. A brief overview for each chapter is given below.

Overview

Chapter 1: The revised Ofsted framework and everyday practice

This chapter gives an overview of the revised Ofsted framework and discusses what it entails and what it means for everyday practice. The chapter also looks at two key areas: British values and school readiness and how these are interpreted for the Foundation Stage and should be part and parcel of everyday provision and organisation. The discussion on school readiness reviews what this means in terms of actual approaches and the wider context of what it entails to be 'ready for school'.

Chapter 2: Getting the basics right

This chapter looks at the need for a common sense of purpose and how to get everyone to commit to shared goals in Reception and in the school as a whole. It offers practical guidance using tried and tested methods on creating a vision statement for your Reception class/es and discusses how it could impact on the whole school vision. It then looks at embedding this vision in your practice, and discusses two key areas: growth mindsets and behaviour for learning.

Chapter 3: Routines and environment

This chapter discusses the importance of getting these routines right so they meet the needs of the children and allow time for in-depth learning to take place and gives some practical advice in implementing routines that allow this to happen. The environment, both physical and emotional, is integral to successful practice and getting them right to meet the ever-changing needs and interests of young learners is central to outstanding practice. In this chapter, both the indoor and outdoor environments are discussed as is the importance of viewing all environments as one coherent learning and teaching space.

Chapter 4: Observation, assessment and planning

This chapter discusses the importance of a robust observational system ensuring that all children are regularly observed when learning and how these observations should immediately feed back into provision and possible extensions. This chapter argues that classroom learning should be driven by observation and accurate assessment.

Chapter 5: Discrete challenges and shared success criteria

This chapter looks in detail at offering children discrete and differentiated challenge and offers practical suggestions on how to implement and monitor them ensuring that provision takes learning forward. This chapter discusses the need for explicit challenge in the Reception class and how teachers can strike a balance between the focus input children require, the self-initiated learning and the challenge element. It looks at shared success criteria and bringing children's voices into the assessment process.

Chapter 6: Progress

This chapter discusses what constitutes good or better progress in the Reception year, and offers practical guidance on tracking children's progress towards and beyond the Early

Learning Goals ensuring that there are regular opportunities for formative assessment and summative planning based upon children's requirements. This chapter stresses the need for high aspirations and expectations for all children so they make good or better progress from their relative starting points.

Chapter 7: Leading an effective Reception class team

This chapter discusses the need for strong and coherent leadership within the Reception class. It looks at the role of the leader and how to develop a confident and capable team who share the same values and vision. This chapter also discusses the role of the leader in monitoring and evaluating the quality of the Reception class so there is a never-ending cycle of improvement in place.

I do hope that you enjoy reading this book and take from it some useful and proven strategies to employ in your schools and classrooms. It has been a privilege to write and I am in awe of the fantastic work that many Reception teachers do for their children – it is a selfless role, constantly giving and reviewing. I wish all Reception teachers the very best in their ceaseless pursuit of developing enquiring minds and excited learners.

1 The revised common inspection framework and everyday practice

'Ofsted' – the very word often strikes fear into the heart of many seasoned and experienced professionals in the Reception class, let alone NQTs and practitioners who are new to the phase. They find themselves caught unwittingly between two stools, wondering: what will the inspectors be looking for? Is it alright if I'm playing with the children? Will they expect to see formal teaching? So many questions result in uncertainty and confusion. Combine this with some schools' unrealistic developmental approach and the outcome can be less than good.

This chapter aims to allay some misconceptions and put the revised framework within the context of everyday practice. You must remember that any inspector is a visitor to your school and is privileged to see you in action and share your time with the children.

Getting to grips with the expectations

I have to admit I was extremely reluctant to include a section on Ofsted within this book because the framework is altered in appearance and wording almost as frequently as I purchase new shoes and so the information available can often be outdated immediately. To paraphrase The Clash: 'All over people changing the framework along with their overcoats'. There seems to be a 'revised edition' coming out at regular intervals, adding, it must be said, much confusion to schools and being used, incorrectly I believe, by schools as their yardstick of 'quality'.

You might say that it is easy for me to say this, but I view Ofsted as the minimum requirement that all schools should be doing well. Too often schools are driven by an Ofsted framework and lose sight of their own agenda as everything is about being 'Ofsted ready'. To me this is a shame, as schools are increasingly being driven by external forces and a limited criteria rather than putting in place rigorous systems themselves and building up an effective pedagogic and reflective approach that is clear, consistent and leads to improved outcomes and greater emotional well-being on behalf of the adults and the children.

But it is what it is, and the latest incarnation of the **Common Inspection Framework** at least goes some way to ensuring that that there is greater equality of judgement and expectation across all sectors of provision.

So what does it all mean and how can you ensure that you have the confidence in your practice to say, 'Yes, thanks for that, now let me show you what we really do exceptionally well'.

There is the concept of 'school readiness' that is bandied about with a relentless intensity but with little guidance or support in defining or understanding, within our culture of 21st century Britain, what this actually means to everyday practice and provision. I will discuss this in more detail on page 24. Schools have sometimes made their own assumptions and taken school readiness to imply compliance, politeness and the ability to sit still and concentrate – as if good learning happens when children are seated and being quiet for prolonged periods of times.

'The most advanced stage of physical development is the ability to sit totally still' (Sally Goddard Blythe, 'First steps to the most important ABC', *TES*)

This is why people practise yoga, for years. Yet we are often asking the youngest of children to sit and be quiet for prolonged periods of time, thus asking them to conform to behaviour and practice that they are neither physically or cognitively ready for. The results of such an approach can lead to early underachievement and a disconnection from the learning experience as many children need to move about to 'get their brains into gear'. The more physically connected a child is, the more the cognitive capacity flows. Young children need to move to connect not only their bodies but also their brains – to get the synapses flying across the brain that strengthen the myelin connectors so learning and skills are embedded. (For further information, see Sally Goddard Blythe in the Bibliography). Young children are sensory creatures, they need to move, to smell things, to touch, taste and use all their senses to make sense of and own the world around them. And, as we know, all children develop differently and at differing rates so a one-cap-fits-all approach will just not work. If we put children under stress with unrealistic expectations the cortisone produced as a result starts to destroy the myelin connectors – this is something we do not want.

You might have also noticed that young children have small necks, and perched upon this thin neck is a heavy head, full of a calorie-eating brain. To have children sitting cross-legged on the floor, often looking up at the practitioner is extremely bad for posture and puts a huge strain on the neck and upper shoulders. Put yourself in this situation, it is Saturday night and your favourite television programme is about to start – do you say to your partner: 'Sweetheart it's about to start, let's sit down on the floor with our legs crossed!'? Of course you don't, you get yourself comfy on the couch, with a few snacks and perhaps a glass of Chablis, so your body is relaxed and you can cognitively engage with what you might be watching or listening to. Children need to be physically comfortable in order to mentally engage, so do ensure your expectations are realistic, it is not about control, it is about facilitating the best learning environments for the children.

A look at the common inspection framework

Details of the judgements Ofsted inspectors are required to make of the Foundation Stage are detailed below/opposite.

How early years settings will be judged

(Ofsted, *Early years inspection handbook*, 2015)

Effectiveness of leadership and management

Inspectors will make a judgement on the effectiveness of leadership and management by evaluating the extent to which leaders, managers and governors:

- demonstrate an ambitious vision, have high expectations for what all children can achieve and ensure high standards of provision and care for children
- improve staff practice, teaching and learning through effective systems for supervision, rigorous performance management and appropriate professional development
- evaluate the quality of the provision and outcomes through robust self-evaluation, taking account of the views of parents and children, and use the findings to develop capacity for sustainable improvement
- provide learning programmes and a curriculum that has suitable breadth, depth and relevance so that it meets any relevant statutory requirements, as well as the needs and interests of children
- successfully plan and manage the curriculum and learning programmes so that all children get a good start and are well prepared for the next stage in their learning, especially being ready for school
- actively promote equality and diversity, tackle poor behaviour towards others, including bullying and discrimination, and narrow any gaps in outcomes between different groups of children
- actively promote British values
- make sure that arrangements to protect children meet all statutory and other government requirements, promote their welfare and prevent radicalisation and extremism.

Inspectors will always report on whether or not arrangements for safeguarding children are effective

Quality of teaching, learning and assessment

Inspectors will make a judgement on the effectiveness of teaching, learning and assessment by evaluating the extent to which:

- teachers, practitioners and other staff have consistently high expectations of what each child can achieve, including the most able and the most disadvantaged
- teachers, practitioners and other staff have a secure understanding of the age group they are working with and have relevant subject knowledge that is detailed and communicated well to children
- assessment information is gathered from looking at what children already know, understand and can do, and is informed by their parents and previous providers as appropriate
- assessment information is used to plan appropriate teaching and learning strategies, including to identify children who are falling behind in their learning or who need additional support, enabling children to make good progress and achieve well
- children understand how to develop as a result of regular interaction and encouragement from staff, and parents understand how their children should progress and how they can contribute to this
- information for parents helps them to understand how children are doing in relation to their age and what they need to do to progress; engagement with parents supports their child's learning
- equality of opportunity and recognition of diversity are promoted through teaching and learning
- teaching supports children to acquire the skills and capacity to develop and learn effectively, and to be ready for the next stages in their learning, especially school where applicable.

[This section is important as it enshrines the 'Characteristics of effective teaching and learning' (see page 9).]

Personal development, behaviour and welfare

Inspectors will make a judgement on the personal development, behaviour and welfare of children by evaluating the extent to which the provision is successfully promoting and supporting children's:

- sense of achievement and commitment to learning through a positive culture that is evident across the whole setting
- self-confidence, self-awareness and understanding of how to be a successful learner
- enjoyment of learning and the development of their independence and ability to explore their surroundings and use their imagination
- social and emotional preparation for their transition within the setting, into other early years settings, and into maintained nursery provision and/or Reception class
- emotional security, through emotional attachments with practitioners and carers, and their physical and emotional health
- prompt and regular attendance
- following of any guidelines for behaviour and conduct, including management of their own feelings and behaviour, and how they relate to others
- understanding of how to keep themselves safe from relevant risks, including when using the internet and social media
- knowledge of how to keep themselves healthy, including through exercising and eating healthily
- personal development, so that they are well-prepared to respect others and contribute to wider society and life in Britain.

Outcomes for children

Inspectors will take account of current levels of development and progress and make a relevant judgement on learning outcomes for children by evaluating the extent to which:

- all children progress well from their different starting points
- children meet or exceed the level of development that is typical for their age so that they can move on to the next stage of their education.

This judgement will then be summarised under the banner of 'Overall effectiveness of the Foundation Stage'.

(Ofsted, *Early years inspection handbook*, 2015)

Inspectors must use all their evidence to evaluate, interestingly and tellingly, what it is like to be a child in the provision. In making their judgements about a provider's overall effectiveness, inspectors will consider whether the standard of education and care is good or whether it exceeds good and is therefore outstanding. If it is not good, inspectors will consider whether it requires improvement or is inadequate.

Inspectors should take account of all the judgements made across the evaluation schedule. In particular, they should consider:

- the progress all children make in their learning and development relative to their starting points and their readiness for the next stage of their education including, where appropriate, readiness for school
- the extent to which the learning and care that the setting provides meet the needs of the range of children who attend, including disabled children and those who have special educational needs
- children's personal and emotional development, including whether they feel safe and are secure and happy
- whether the requirements for children's safeguarding and welfare have been fully met and there is a shared understanding of and responsibility for protecting children
- the effectiveness of leadership and management in evaluating practice and securing continuous improvement that improves children's life chances.

(Ofsted, *Early years inspection handbook*, 2015)

So how do you contextualise all this?

I suggest a rigorous audit. It might seem slightly mad, but I always look at the inadequate judgements as a basis for this. Are any of these in evidence in your audit? If the answer is no, and it should be, then you can move forward. This is not to say that you are driven by Ofsted, but it is there and it is not going to go away. So the sooner you have an understanding and ownership of the documentation, the less daunting the process will be for you and your team.

The audit table on the opposite page is an excellent starting point to ensure that all the evidence is in place and you are confident in talking about your impact on children's learning and outcomes – I shall be discussing this in greater depth in Chapter 7, page 105.

Strands	Evidence in policy and practice Have you evidence for:	Actions to implement	Monitoring: by whom and when	Milestones: when are elements to be completed	Evaluation and next steps
Leadership	• Shared vision? • CPD and impact? • Performance management linked to outcomes for children? • Monitoring and action planning? • How the gap is narrowing between identified groups? • Parental and children's contributions? • Safeguarding procedures? • Strategic development plan?				
Teaching and learning	• Monitoring the quality of teaching? • Curriculum and developmental maps? • Use of assessment to plan for individual needs?				
Personal and social	• The impact of clear transition processes? • Attendance figures and processes to improve attendance? • Children's ability to self-regulate? • Children's ability to talk about their learning? • Independent learning?				
Outcomes	• On entry assessments? • Analysis of progress for all children? • Impact of targeted interventions? • Planning being driven by assessment and observation and meeting the needs of the children? • Regular analysis of progress and planned support? • Raised outcomes for all children and figures that are above the national average?				

Figure 1. Initial auditing and action planning

British values

This is a difficult area for many schools, as this is often covered through a rigorous Personal, Social and Emotional Development (PSED) curriculum. In many schools I have visited I have seen display boards festooned with the Union Jack flag with huge lettering all over. To me, they look odd and slightly scary! I just don't think that we are used to this, because our values and principles are firmly embedded and we do what we do as a result of hundreds of years of developing democracy, tolerance and respect – trying to tie down British values is extremely difficult. But let's be realistic about what this means for this age group in the Foundation Stage.

The Foundation Years website has produced an extremely useful document which will greatly assist in putting a complex issue into context (www.foundationyears.org.uk/files/2015/03/Fundamental_British_Values.pdf).

Below I look at each section briefly – and what they might and realistically, should, look and feel like in your classrooms. It is about giving the children the opportunity to act out.

Democracy

What opportunities do you provide for children to make decisions and build their self-esteem and positive mindset? This involves the balance of decision-making as a whole group. The 'what makes a good…' question is a useful device here i.e what makes a good learner, teacher, friend? This shared success criteria will result in an agreed way of working and behaving in the classroom – it will take time as children move from a more ego-centric perspective to one of greater understanding of the needs of others. It is important that, over time, children see themselves as part of the wider classroom and that their actions may have a positive or detrimental effect on others.

In reality, this strand underpins the PSED aspects of the EYFS and the 'Characteristics of effective teaching and learning', whereby children are an active part of the decision-making processes. From this, confidence will increase and children will gain the strength of character to realise that they also have a contribution to make, that their voices and opinions add value to the workings of the classroom. It is important from an adult perspective, to encourage questioning; the use of open-ended discussions and possibility thinking strongly support this area. It is also well worth standing back and asking – how much democracy is there in evidence in the classroom? Some practitioners do find this hard, as they might see it as a lessening of adult authority in the classroom which takes them out of their comfort zone. What you are trying to achieve here is the concept of autonomy – which links to Rule of law (see below).

Rule of law

This concerns the development of agreed codes of conduct and expectation in the classroom – not always, I stress, from an adult to child perspective, but also from a child to adult view – how we share ideas and resources and how we agree what is acceptable and what is not in terms of overall behaviour. You have to tread a careful path here to ensure that you do not offend cultural sensitivities as in modern Britain there a numerous cultures and faiths to take into consideration. One of the most positive examples of this I have witnessed is at Oakington Manor Primary School in Wembley. The school is next to Wembley Stadium in the heart of a rich and diverse community. Within the school boundaries there is clear understanding on behalf of all stakeholders as to how the school runs, and the expectations on all, regardless of cultural background. The school cannot replicate the trials and strife of the wider world, but it can inculcate a wider acceptance of difference and similarities. St. Mary's Catholic Infant School in Croydon summarises this point very succinctly: their aim is 'being kind'. This simple message underscores a plethora of messages and creates an innate understanding of how children should operate in the school and what their responsibilities are. Agreement of shared rules in the classroom start at a very simple level, for example in a Reception context, I see putting lids on pens (my bug bear!) as good evidence of the Rule of Law.

Individual liberty

It should be the aim of every school to help children develop a positive sense of themselves and a can-do attitude working autonomously within a shared and agreed framework. Routines and expectations must provide meaningful opportunities for all children to develop their confidence in their own abilities, and in talking about their experiences and learning. I will return to this important issue later in the book when I discuss the 'Learning detective' and 'Working wall' concepts (page 68). As a teacher in the Reception class, you should provide a range of opportunities and experiences that will allow children to explore the language of feelings and responsibility, and start to understand that everybody might have different opinions, but they are all valued within the context of the school.

Mutual respect and tolerance of different faiths and beliefs

How do you do this in your classroom? This might be especially difficult if the intake of your school is mono-cultural, as you do not want to pay lip service to other cultures and beliefs by briefly covering them when certain festivals might appear on the calendar. It is vital that children in schools where there is a predominant culture are exposed to the beliefs of others in an engaging and meaningful way, otherwise we are doing our children a great disservice and not preparing them for the future – it is not good enough just to make clay divas at Diwali. This strand is predominantly about preparing children for life beyond the school gates in modern Britain, where they will be surrounded by sights, smells, sounds and cultures that might be significantly different from their own.

It might be that you have to reach beyond your immediate community and make positive relationships with other faith or cultural schools. This needs to be done in order for children to gain an appreciation of the wider world, so that they acquire a deep tolerance, appreciation and respect for their own and other cultures. Children should know about similarities and differences between themselves and others, with a great stress being laid upon the similarity – too often the differences are highlighted and there is not enough work on what is the same – and the underlying principles of goodness and kindness to others.

All of these are covered by the Communication and Language, Understanding the World and PSED aspects of the Foundation Stage .You will not be expecting your children to have lengthy discussions concerning the problems of the world, although they would probably come up with some far more sensible suggestions in how to deal with them – what you will need to ensure is that there is ample evidence in your everyday practice to ensure that children are given time and opportunity to:

- give their views
- value and respect the views of others
- take turns, collaborate and share
- ask question to develop enquiring minds
- develop self-esteem and confidence in their own ability
- explore the language of feelings, responsibility and different opinions.

Throughout the course of the book I shall be offering suggestions and proven strategies that will assist in ensuring all the bases are covered in detail and the principles just become part and parcel of your everyday practice.

School readiness

This is, and always has been, a very controversial area and can be interpreted differently from school to school. In my view, a school's interpretation of school readiness is inextricably linked to its vision of what constitutes good learning and its values concerning behaviour (which will be discussed in detail in Chapter 2, page 31). For a far more theoretical discussion I would strongly recommend that you access the The Unicef document: *School Readiness: a Conceptual Framework* (www.unicef.org/education/files/Chil2Child_ConceptualFramework_FINAL(1).pdf).

As a professional, I have never truly understood or embraced the concept of school readiness. We do not have 'nursery readiness' or 'Reception readiness'. What we do have is overarching expectations of where children should be developmentally at certain milestones, which consequently allows teachers and schools to develop appropriate provision and high aspirations. This is understandable given that all humans develop at differing rates and at different times, sometimes rapidly and sometimes at a slower burn level. This is the key, children do not develop the same skills and knowledge at the same time – so the whole definition of school readiness really concerns the individual children and what schools are going to provide for them in their years following the Foundation Stage to ensure that they are able to access the curriculum on equal terms.

School readiness as a concept hints at the suggestion that the Foundation Stage, and Reception in particular, are mere stepping stones in the preparation for 'school proper' and this approach is still, unfortunately, the driving force and all too prevalent and persuasive in many of our schools where good learning is seen as quiet and compliant children, sitting at tables. Some baseline systems for entry to Reception do utilise or stress approaches that concentrate on literacy and numeracy, and this can have a detrimental effect on the provision and practice that is afforded to the children – a narrowing of the focus. It is easy to see why this might be the case, it is far easier to measure progress in literacy and numeracy than in PSED and children's dispositions to learn. Whilst this somewhat narrow skills and knowledge focus would align with a primary school curriculum, there needs to be a far greater focus and discussion within schools on the wider concept of learning and understanding how children learn. I find it odd that this narrow approach remains persistent in many of our schools despite a revised curriculum that is now more in line with the sound pedagogic approaches of the Foundation Stage and one which focuses mainly on 'embedded learning' throughout the subsequent year groups.

I hate to be difficult, but why not? Children from birth are learning at an alarming rate and if schools and practitioners are fully aware of where a child is developmentally and subsequently provide resources and expectations that are developmentally appropriate, then the children will be ready for that next step. The message here is to analyse where the children are, what are the gaps in learning and understanding and focus on these to ensure that school readiness is not an issue – it is about being realistic!

You are not going to get class of 30 or more children to the same place at the end of the summer term in Reception – why? Because they are all unique and individual!

I read a poster in a Reception class at Green Vale Infants in Chatham, which stated:

'All children come bearing gifts, they just unwrap them at different times.'

This speaks volumes for the understanding within the school concerning the link between a ready child and a ready school.

It is the aspiration of schools that children achieve and attain as well as they can so that they have the confidence to tackle their next academic or social challenges with confidence in themselves as a capable learner. This, of course, cannot be carried out by the school or class teacher in isolation, and the relationship the school fosters with parents and carers is crucial in understanding the holistic child and consequently providing a physical and emotional environment that is conducive to deep-level learning.

National data for 2015 shows that: '66.3% of children achieved a good level of development' at the end of the Reception Year (*Early Years Foundation Stage Profile Results in England*, 2015 DfE). This means that nearly 34% of children did not! Also, it must be remembered, that within the 'expected' band there is a vast disparity of ability because the final judgement at the end of the Foundation Stage is a 'best fit' and children do not have to have total mastery of each statement within the goal. Some children might be extremely confident within the goal, others less so, but, as a 'best fit' from teacher judgement, they all will have achieved the early learning goal. The differential here could be vast. For those 34% of children who did not attain the Early Learning Goals, it is vital that the teachers in the following year group have a clear picture of where, developmentally, these children sit so they can offer them an environment and routines that are developmentally and cognitively appropriate.

The physical environment, curriculum content and modes of delivery in KS1 – the routines and physical space to allow all areas of learning to be covered and not primarily focused on the narrow parameters of numeracy and literacy – is something that needs to be developed in many schools. Great schools appreciate that all areas of learning are of equal worth and that to compartmentalise learning and specific subjects into time-bonded sessions does not allow for a breadth of learning and application opportunities. Curriculum development is vital here. In the Foundation Stage, practitioners are providing for 17 areas of learning simultaneously, safe and secure in the knowledge that numeracy and literacy can occur and be taught and assessed in a multitude of areas and ways and not necessarily only during a focused session.

There is an interesting development point here with many schools now looking at their infant and junior timetables because their current practice is no longer fit for purpose. The breadth of learning required through the revised curriculum must result in a re-assessment of the learning day. During many a school visit and undertaking scrutinies in Years 1 and 2, I see so much unfinished and incomplete work in numeracy and literacy books. This, in essence, is a reflection of the ineffective and inappropriate pedagogic approach that is being adopted in many schools, and mirrors the lack of cohesion in the whole learning journey and indeed the lack of connectivity in learning for the children.

I would just ask you to put yourselves in the shoes of a five- or six-year-old and consider a sample morning...

After listening to the focused literacy input you are then required to undertake some work, either independently or with an adult. Then it's time to put your books away and line up for 'play time'. You then run around on a bit of flat tarmac (not a lot of play involved), get hot and sweaty, perhaps fall over or get struck by a rogue ball. Then it's back to the classroom and you have to switch your brain into numeracy mode – thinking that you have yet to complete the literacy challenge. Where are the connections and where is the time afforded to practise and embed in meaningful cross-curricula ways?

As a slight aside, but still addressing the same point. I find it ludicrous and somewhat depressing that we take away greater independence and meaningful play/learning opportunities in the infants when the children are able to show and display all these characteristics in abundance as a result of solid Foundation Stage practice with an emphasis on the 'Characteristics of effective teaching and learning' (see page 9).

Questions for reflection

- What do the 'Characteristics of effective teaching and learning' look like in your school in the years following the Foundation Stage?
- What processes are in place to ensure that all three Characteristics hold firm in subsequent years and are firmly embedded in a shared and responsible pedagogic approach?

It is worth noting, however, that at a time when there is great emphasis on inculcating British values in schools there seems to be an increasing desire by the DfE to look abroad for approaches that will supposedly assist in raising outcomes for children. Looking at different nations whose cultures and views on childhood and educational techniques might be different from ours is surely a recipe for disaster and confusion. On the one hand, we have leaders in industry decrying the fact that there are not enough capable independent, resilient problem-solvers leaving the school system, and on the other we are adopting practices that are more akin to hot housing, compliance and drilling and a one-cap-fits-all approach, rather than deep level thinking and reflection, to raise standards; which will entail a far deeper understanding of what learning is about. There is a dichotomy in purpose and approach here and this is adding to the confusion and frustration many schools and leadership teams feel.

I feel that there is correctly a focus on core and basic skills – without these, children will not be able to operate freely and productively in their later lives and this is surely down to 'quality first teaching' within a culture that is reflective of wider society and society's aims and ambitions. My main concern is with the approaches employed to achieve this – narrowing the focus and concentrating on core skills much to detriment of what it entails to be a learner in school and beyond. I remember my dear old grandmother saying to me: 'School, Neil, is not about learning facts, it is about learning to learn for life' – thanks Gran, I have taken your philosophy with me.

What we have briefly touched upon here is the symbiotic relationship between school readiness and the readiness of schools for children. The two are inseparable and must be addressed. If there is a disconnection in learning and teaching approaches, philosophies and pedagogy between the phases, it will invariably result in confusion for teachers, pupils and families. The move towards a more 'formal' top down approach is often seen as a positive development in many schools, as if the key message is: 'Well they (the children) have had a couple of years of playing, now the real learning happens'. This, I will argue long into the night, is total and complete nonsense.

Real school readiness –what this looks like in practice

School readiness is not really some abstract concept, it is developmental. With sensitive guidance and support the majority of children will be ready for their next step, but not all at the same time and this is an important point to remember. School readiness is a continuous process as children progress through the Reception year, good schools and teachers consistently raise aspirations and expectations throughout the year so there is no sudden change of emphasis. A great example of this follows.

It was the second half of the summer term and I was visiting Wayfield Primary in Chatham, a newly appointed FS lead was in place who was, and is, an inspiration to both the staff and the children. A sound pedagogic understanding was in place within the school, shared between the Foundation Stage and Year 1, and I wrote the following in the subsequent visit note.

Visit note: Wayfield Primary School, Chatham

Behaviour for learning in the Reception class is outstanding. Children are highly involved in independent learning and the turning of the classroom into an Indian Restaurant to supplement the 'Foods from everywhere' theme was inspirational. Children were confidently playing in role, utilising descriptive and expressive language, experiencing and talking about the different taste sensations, some of which they may not have experienced previously – this widening of children's horizons and experiences is outstanding.

Independent writing was strongly in evidence, particularly for the boys, which was extremely encouraging as the writing experiences were meaningful and fun, supported by key words and vocabulary. Children were taking turns in taking telephone orders and asking clients what they would like to eat, writing down these orders, using phonic knowledge to make plausible attempts at spelling unfamiliar words and using the prompts in the 'restaurant' for key vocabulary. Children were assisting each other in their writing – 'you need to sound it out' was frequently heard. This was first-rate provision and practice.

The learning was excellently supported and modelled by the adults in the room. Expectations on behaviour and language are extremely high and the children have responded positively to, and benefitted greatly from, this security and consistency of expectation from all staff members.

Children are eager to share their learning and what they have been doing – particularly pleasing is the growth in independence within the children and the development of autonomy with children following the routines and expectations because they understand the reasons why and are a full part of the process – they are consequently far more attuned to the needs of others. The school leadership has worked hard on raising the aspirations of all stakeholders and as a result, the children view themselves as learners who are an integral part of the process and are now ready, intrinsically, academically and socially, for their next step in learning and development. There are a small number of children who have not yet reached this stage of development, but support plans are in place to assist them when moving into KS1.

The key brilliance behind what I saw in that class was a true understanding of children who are ready for school and dedication to ensuring environments, routines and expectations were ready, and pitched at the correct level, for these children so they could challenge themselves at a higher level. This in my mind is what school readiness is all about. This definition might require reflection from year to year because children are not all at the same place at the same time from year to year, but the aspiration and methodology remain constant.

School readiness in a mixed cohort

In classes with a mixed cohort, the concept of school readiness is not as clear-cut. It is difficult to establish the same practice discussed above because teachers here will be dealing with Reception and Year 1 aged children in the same learning environment. It is impossible to have two distinct pedagogic approaches in operation in the same physical space, so in attempting to achieve this you would run yourself into the ground and achieve high cortisone levels – so schools in this situation need to make hard and fast decisions as to the approach the learning and teaching will follow. Two schools I have worked with, Warren Mead Infants in Banstead and Surrey Hills C of E Primary School in Dorking, have successfully surmounted the issue of differentiation and school readiness by being clear and consistent in the expectations within the classroom.

Planning using two 'curriculums' is extremely difficult and this is where excellent diagnosis of the actual true level of development of the children in the class comes to the fore. Planning here is based upon detailed analysis of what individuals or groups need in order to make progress, so consequently there is no set formula for teaching. All members of the team are involved in the observation and assessment cycle. What these two schools do extremely well is ensure that there is consistency in approach to learning and teaching – great stress is laid upon differentiated independent challenge and strategic precision teaching, regardless of age, and with hugely high aspirations for all children. Teaching here is pitched at a higher level so Reception children are exposed to higher order thinking and language – as a result the Reception children achieve and attain very well. For those children in Year 1 still operating at or below the Early Learning Goals, there is safety and emotional security in the consistent approaches and expectations. For those who might be deemed 'more able', there is sufficient challenge to ensure that they are given ample opportunities to apply learning in meaningful ways.

What is interesting in both these schools, is that there is no discussion about 'school readiness', there is more of a discussion on the school and the classes being ready for the children and the new cohort. Curriculum and skills development mapping drives the practice forward – the environments are enabling and challenging and children are afforded time to practise and embed new knowledge and skills at various levels. The transition and learning is seamless – when observing the children, one cannot tell the difference between the Reception and Year 1 children when they are independently working – one can tell, however, the difference through the differentiation in expectation. The schools work hard with families to reassure the Year 1 parents that their children will be challenged and consequently will make the required progress, and more.

Summary

In this chapter I have looked at the Ofsted requirements for the Foundation Stage as they currently stand, and hoped to clarify what this might look like in everyday practice. It must be remembered that there is no requirement to teach in a certain way in Reception, what is required is that any approaches adopted add value to the children and their families, enshrine the key principles of the Foundation Stage and assist children in making the best progress that they possibly can from their relative starting points – so it is an amalgamation of many things, all of which form the basis for the next chapters:

- Routines that allow children time and space to practise their developing skills and knowledge in meaningful contexts.
- Enabling environments – both indoors and out.
- Adult engagement in the learning and teaching process – a sensible balance of targeted focus work and independent challenge.
- How your observation and assessment processes result in improved and meaningful planning and provision for groups and individuals.
- All of the above working in unison to ensure that progress in your classroom is outstanding.

I have also discussed the complicated and often divisive topic that is 'school readiness' and the basis for ensuring approaches remain constant throughout the school. In short, the approach to learning and teaching should remain constant, what changes as the children grow and gain confidence is the challenge and the expectation.

2 Getting the basics right

It's important to go back to the basics to determine the long-term aim of what you're trying to achieve. Too often schools look at the minute detail (e.g. phonic schemes, progress in number, interventions and displays) and focus too readily upon them, consequently awareness of the bigger picture gets lost somewhere in translation. I would argue that the true premise here is to take a step back from the chalk face and look at the bigger picture and ask, 'What are we doing and why? Is our current philosophy and approach meeting the wider needs of the community and ensuring there is clear strategic direction which allows the children to achieve as best as they can?'.

Leadership here is vital in providing direction for the class and the team in order to influence and develop fellow professionals. This chapter looks in detail at the role of leadership in developing and articulating a collective vision which will ensure that there is a shared understanding and goals for all stakeholders – including parents.

The way that you behave and conduct yourself in the classroom everyday has the greatest impact on promoting children's dispositions to learn and also in motivating and inspiring your team. Your behaviour and vision dictates and reflects the mood of the room, which feeds in to how the children learn, how they view themselves as learners, how the adults work alongside the children, and even the relationships with parents.

Working with young children and their families requires an outstanding set of personal qualities. It is without doubt one of the hardest jobs in education – you need to be passionate and professional, empathetic and understanding, have high expectations of all stakeholders that are realistic and achievable, and ensure everybody holds onto the same overall goals or else the ship starts to let in water at an alarming rate.

Developing an overall strategic vision for your Reception class

There are four key elements to consider when putting together an overall strategic vision for your Reception classes.

1. **Forging the class direction** – this key area of class or phase leadership involves the practice of identifying and, with the team, creating an agreed set of objectives and a shared way of working. This is done through:

   - agreeing, identifying and articulating the shared vision

   - ensuring there is a genuine passion for, and understanding of, early years education

   - identifying shared understanding and common language so there are no misinterpretations

   - putting in place open and transparent systems of communication between all stakeholders

   - being self-reflective, thoughtful, and empathetic to the stages of development of all stakeholders.

2. **Developing a constructive workforce** – any success in the classroom or school is totally dependent upon the high level of commitment and energy shown by all the members of the team. This endeavour and energy should be recognised and promoted by the leader who also identifies the potential of individuals to improve or take on added responsibilities. This is done through:

   - a commitment to the ongoing professional development and the identification of CPD opportunities for all staff members – I would also include lunchtime supervisors in this

   - emphasising the importance of all adult's roles in the learning process. There are often misconceptions about the work that is carried out in the Reception class; it is seen as playing about, and in certain instances I have come across practitioners who see deployment in the Reception class as a demotion in standing within the school because it does not entail 'proper teaching' – this is unforgivable and shows a total lack of understanding of what the complex role of a Reception teacher entails

   - a focus on the learning and teaching within the classrooms and outdoors and an agreed pedagogic approach to learning and teaching

   - a rigorous monitoring system and the linking of staff appraisal to children's progress

   - leadership acting as a positive role model to all staff

   - being able to influence others within the learning community in a purposeful and intrinsic way.

3. **Developing the Foundation Stage and Infants as a cohesive unit** – there needs to be a commitment to developing the Foundation Stage within a school, and here I would stress the importance of external links with providers and significantly the infants within the school, as a cohesive learning and teaching community. Leadership is required to build positive relationships between all the key players, including governors and external agencies. This is done through:

- collaborative building of a shared learning community within the school – sharing best strategies and providing free access to information
- facilitating and encouraging community links – who in the local community can offer you more opportunities and experiences for the children that might not be readily to hand in the classroom
- the promotion of a professional and caring environment – one that is inclusive and pays due attention to the needs of individuals within the structure
- the positive demonstration and engagement of leadership and management skills in continual and rigorous professional development.

4. **Ensuring the 'Characteristics of Effective Teaching and Learning' (see page 9) are at the very heart of your practice in the Reception class and enshrined, modelled and understood by all stakeholders**– the focus here is on inculcating growth mindsets (page 41) within the adults who are supporting the children and the children themselves so that adults are supporting children's motivation and interests. This is done through:

- Sensitive participation in play – following the lead and extending the learning taking place
- Genuine interest that encourages the development of language (see Chapter 7, page 105)
- Acknowledgement of success and ideas with specific comments to develop language and reasoning skills, the ability to self-reflect and ways in which to improve – leading to the development of 'behaviour for learning' (see Chapter 7, page 105).

You might like to fill in the table below to consider whether the three 'Characteristics of effective teaching and learning' are thoroughly embedded in your Reception class, and if not, what you could do to make improvements.

Characteristic of effective teaching and learning	What we currently do and is evident in our practice	What we can improve upon and when/whom to lead	Impact and review of improvements
Playing and exploring			
Active learning			
Creating and thinking critically			

Figure 2. How well are the 'Characteristics of effective teaching and learning' embedded in your practices?

Leadership qualities

Each of the four elements described above requires a differing set of leadership qualities.

In their book, *Effective and Caring Leadership in the Early Years*, Iram Siraj- and Elaine Hallet identify four themes of leadership and subsequent practices;

Themes of leadership	Expertise within the themes
Directional leadership	Developing a shared vision Effective Communication
Collaborative leadership	Promoting a team culture Promoting parental contributions
Empowering leadership	The processes of change Promoting agency
Pedagogical leadership	Leading learning Reflective learning

This table refers to directional leadership and collaborative elements.

Practical task: setting your vision

If we consider the first element: 'Forging the class direction' (page 32), as a lead teacher in the Reception class you will need to direct the vision of learning, teaching, assessment and planning, as forming this agreement will ensure that everything else falls into place, or conversely falls apart if there is not sound and purposeful agreement in the direction the class or unit is moving.

Vision is an important and some would say, critical, feature of effective and purposeful directional leadership. Any vision needs to be clearly articulated, shared, agreed and be intrinsically linked to the particular needs and priorities of both the EYFS and the immediate community. To achieve any set outcomes or desired developments a clear vision must exist. Without a clearly articulated vision those working within the Foundation Stage might be working towards different and conflicting agendas, often led by their interpretation of what Foundation Stage practice should look and feel like, rather than by a shared vision and agreement that has been ascertained through consultation, research and a consideration of the school context.

Key questions for leaders when developing the vision

- What are the current educational and social influences upon your vision (research, experience, development)?
- How is your vision going to be articulated to stakeholders?

- How do you ensure that this vision becomes collective, shared and agreed?
- How does your vision mirror and support your personal leadership style, so that you are not compromising yourself?

Effective leaders inspire others with a vision of a better future and provide a focus for development and growth within a school or classroom. The leader's capacity to clearly articulate and evidence a shared vision that is owned by all and linked to the key issues within the school or class is imperative.

Leithwood and Riehl (2003) argue that the 'providing of direction' is one of the two overarching functions of quality leadership – it is the responsibility of the leader or leaders to shape, determine and articulate the vision and to make that vision a reality. It is crucial that leadership possesses an intrinsic and detailed understanding of the needs and aspirations of the children and families in their schools – I would add to this that the role also entails, in many cases, the raising of these aspirations.

A very effective way of promoting and agreeing this 'togetherness' and sense of purpose is to undertake the following task about setting out your vision.

This process encourages practitioners and stakeholders to evaluate their practice and views, and considering:

- are they in line with statutory requirements?
- is there ample opportunity for children to build up the Characteristics of Effective Learning?
- are we promoting British values?

Background information about the task

I have been working with school leadership teams all over the country for many years on this process. The impact is very impressive because it goes beyond the obvious and looks at the long-term aim of the Reception class, which should of course be tied in with the whole school vision. It is interesting to note that as a result of this process many schools have in fact revisited their whole school statement and vision to ensure that it is based upon the solid foundations from their Early Years vision. They have come to the conclusion that there is no point in drilling down and laying blocks on uneasy footings, it is far more constructive to build from the bottom up – obvious really, you don't start with the roof when building a house do you?

I shall be drawing on my experience of working with and supporting schools and leaders up and down the country – in many instances going right back to the basics, and putting forward suggestions and strategies that will assist you in gaining an ownership of your classroom and a true understanding of your vital role as a facilitator, mediator and coach in young children's acquisition of learning. It is not a one-cap-fits-all solution, but rather some practical tips that you may wish to employ, alter and make your own.

I have worked with a large number of schools on this process. Six schools went about this process in very similar ways and I shall be drawing on these examples when discussing the task: Iqra Primary School in Slough, St. Mary's Catholic Infant School in Croydon, Moss

Lane School in Godalming, Park Mead Primary in Cranleigh, Riverley Primary School in Leyton and Hamsey Green Primary School in Warlingham.

All these schools have in place excellent directional leadership that has greatly assisted in developing a shared vision for the entire school and backed this up by having exceptional and effective communication channels. They also actively encouraged the parents to come into the classrooms at the beginning of the day as they see this community link and transparency as vitally important to involving parents and carers in the learning process.

Iqra Primary School, Slough

This school is a truly wondrous place where learning is explicit everywhere, expectations and aspirations are incredibly high, and leadership develops skills and attributes within all staff members.

The Reception team work closely across the three classrooms and outdoor zone – continually reflecting on practice and provision. Together they share strengths within the team, areas to develop and aspirations. The display photographed opposite is in a prominent position within the unit and is visible by all stakeholders. It is this continued review and reflection that ensures the children and families within the school are afforded the very best possible practice.

What I also like about the school is that they celebrate the small achievements of the staff members through the 'proud cloud' concept. The view being that they celebrate children's achievements through this process, and they are part of the Foundation Stage family, so let's celebrate what we do well too. This continued acknowledgement of good practice by professional peers, e.g. it could be that a story was brilliantly read, the outdoor opportunities are first class, or the phonics session went particularly well, has resulted in a real sense of purpose, pride and direction.

Setting the vision: carrying out the task

In all the schools mentioned here, the SLT and governors were involved from the outset. They were consulted initially about the purpose and process of the activity, which was:

- to have a shared agreement on how the children will learn in the Reception classes
- the attributes they hope the learners in the Reception classes would develop and how this pedagogic approach would then be carried on through the Infants and into KS2 – putting the Characteristics of Effective Learning and Teaching firmly on the school agenda, especially 'creativity and critical thinking'.

Photo 1. Display in Reception unit in Iqra Primary School, Slough

The onus was very much on inculcating independent, autonomous learners. This process assisted in underpinning the whole school mission statement, breaking it down into constituent parts, and focused on how the vision can become enshrined in everyday practice and provision.

The parents and carers were then involved. They were invited to a specially convened parents' meeting where they were informed of the process and how the school places high value on parental partnership, by the Foundation Stage lead, chair of governors and the headteacher.

Following the meeting, which in all schools was extraordinarily well-attended, a display board was set up in a location where parents had access, showing a big circle with the words, 'We are revisiting our vision – can you help?' in the middle, and words to select around the outside (see below: this is not a definitive list; when you do this do add some of your own).

Parents and all stakeholders were then invited to place words that they consider important in the circle. However, the key thing here is that you are only allowed six words in the circle at any one time – I call this the 'circle of trust' as all stakeholders are entrusting their views to others.

Figure 3. Circle of trust

Adventurous	Energetic
Affectionate	Fearful
Good at guessing	Friendly
Asks questions	Industrious
Athletic	Independent
Careful	Negative
Conforming	Obedient
Competitive	Quiet
Co-operative	Rebellious
Courageous	Refined
Courteous	Receptive
Creative	Risk taking
Critical	Self-confident
Domineering	Self-satisfied
Emotional	Sensitive
Has a sense of humour	Timid
Stubborn	Versatile
Talkative	Well-adjusted
Resilient	Problem solving
Persistent	Empathetic

After a three week period the words in the centre will be pretty much established. All stakeholders will have had their say on what characteristics they would like to see the children exhibiting by the end of the Reception Year.

It is important to note here that these are also the characteristics you would wish to see all staff members exhibiting. It is also worth physically drawing a line through those characteristics you would not wish to encourage, or your setting currently encourages. Are there any questions this throws up in line with your vision? If so what are you going to do about it?

Once you have done this, you now have your key ingredients in place. Get these enshrined in a big display format, e.g. 'Children at our school are learning to be...' Supplement this with pictures that highlight these characteristics.

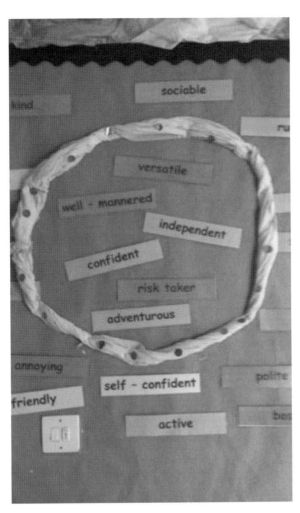

Photo 2. Circle of trust in action at Iqra Primary School. Shared and agreed by all stakeholders.

Now the fun begins ...

If, for example, you have agreed upon:

- Creative
- Resilient
- Co-operative
- Self-confident
- Empathetic
- Adventurous

All of these will have to be unpicked, reviewed and restructured. This is exciting as you will now have ownership of the Reception class, you will be driving practice and thinking forward. These agreed values will also become part of your appraisal system. A key point here is that if you have all agreed on the statements, then all the team will have to display and model them in great detail and depth.

The whole of your practice will have to mirror these, including your:

- Routines
- Planning
- Assessment and observational systems
- Physical environment
- Role as a support for children
- Learning and teaching strategies.

It is also useful, as a team exercise, to ensure that there are like-minded people within the team. Sometimes you might inherit a team who has been in post for many years and

Photo 3. The vision enshrined at Hamsey Green Primary School, Warlingham

can be somewhat set in their ways, it is important to get these people on side. Often I have found that there can be two types of person working in Reception classes – more often 'radiators'; who are vibrant, exciting, sensitive and stimulating, and, sometimes, 'drains'; need we say anymore. Reception classes cannot afford to have staff who could be perceived as 'drains' working within them. So these agreed values also need to become part and parcel of the appraisal system so all practitioners are living and acting out the vision and values everyday.

From vision to practice

Your action/development plans and the subsequent policies that evolve and develop through your vision are part of the processes and procedures that you will need to implement in order to provide effective directional leadership in a planned and purposeful way, and ensure that the aims and objectives of the vision exercise are agreed, met and reviewed on a regular basis. This does not call for fundamental change, but some fine-tuning might be needed once the operation starts in earnest.

Policy is the process of documenting the framework of a cohesive delivery of the curriculum, the safeguarding of children, and includes equality and well-being. The action plans developed following the vision statement exercise will provide a format and framework for implementing this vision into everyday practice and include a manageable, time-bonded system for review. A key question to ask is this: if a visitor walked into your classroom, would the vision and organisation be clear to them, and how would it be articulated?

One of the key ways that the vision and subsequent action plans can be articulated, is through the everyday practice on show: the involvement of children, the engagement of the adults, the independence, the language, the enabling environments and the purposeful learning opportunities available to the children.

Growth mindsets

The concept of a growth mindset was developed by psychologist Carol Dweck and popularised in her book, *Mindset* (2012) In recent years, many schools and educational leaders have started using Dweck's theories to inform how they teach children in their schools, this is profoundly so in the Foundation Stage, where this philosophy has for years been an unwritten way of working with young children.

A mindset, according to Dweck, is a self-perception or 'self-theory' that people hold about themselves. Believing that you are either 'intelligent' or 'unintelligent' is a simple example of a mindset. People may also have a mindset related to either or both their personal or professional lives, e.g. I'm a good athlete or I'm a bad mathematician. People can often be aware or unaware of their mindsets, according to Dweck, but they can have a profound effect on learning achievement, skill acquisition, personal relationships, professional success, and many other dimensions of life.

Dweck's work centres on the central distinction between a 'fixed' and a 'growth' mindset. According to Dweck, those in a fixed mindset understand personality traits, such as intelligence and talent/ skill, are unchangeable and so 'they spend their time documenting their intelligence or talent instead of developing them. They also believe that talent alone creates success – without effort.'

Dweck's research suggests that people who have adopted a fixed mindset – the belief that they are either clever or not and there is no way to alter this – may learn less and at a slower rate. At the same time they are likely to avoid involving themselves in anything too challenging, since a poor outcome might either confirm they can't learn or indicate that they are less capable than they think, if indeed they do believe they are capable. This is an important point when giving children feedback on their competencies as a learner; too often we shower young children with unwarranted praise just for doing what they should be doing.

This might sound mean, but in my view any praise should be earned and not doled out as part and parcel of everyday conversation.

Empathy and understanding of the 'unique child' is key, hence the need for partnerships, so that any conversations develop the thinking and reasoning skills of the child. It is a matter of engaging with the limbic brain. This part of the brain stores memories of a lifetime and is susceptible to the sensory approach. It also likes to know that it is doing a good job, so sensitive, warranted and meaningful praise are vital in order to keep it going and growing. This praise is especially true when talking to young children. Many adults feel that this is what they should be doing, and therefore there is an inordinate amount of worthless praise thrown about in Reception classes: 'Wonderful, brilliant, well done, aren't you clever?' are phrases I hear time and time again, but they offer little in terms of value added to the learning. If you add on a, 'Have you thought about?' or 'Do you think...?' at the end of the praise, suddenly you are operating in a different dimension of thinking – one of possibility, openness and creativity. I would urge you to change your questioning from 'What is...?' to 'What if...?' – this really changes the direction and enhances the quality of adult – child engagement.

Dweck's findings also suggest that when people with fixed mindsets fail at something, as they inevitably will, they tend to tell themselves that they can't or won't be able to do it, or they make excuses to rationalise the failure, e.g. 'I would have passed the test if I had had more time to study.' This 'could have, should have, would have' mentality often results in a profound 'did not' at the close of the day, and often a deep sense of regret and remorse in later years.

Alternatively, in a growth mindset, people believe that their most basic abilities can be developed through dedication and hard work – brains and any natural talent are just the starting point for further development. Carol Dweck suggests that this 'creates a love of learning and a resilience that is essential for great accomplishment.'

People who embrace growth mindsets – the belief that they can learn more or become smarter if they work hard and persevere – may learn more, learn it more quickly, and view challenges and failures as opportunities to improve their learning and skills.

This difference between a fixed and growth mindset has far-reaching implications for schools, leaders and teachers. It centres on the ways in which children think about their learning, their supposed intelligence, and their own abilities, and can have a significant effect on learning, achievement, overall attainment, and lifelong potential. If schools encourage their children to believe that they can learn more and improve if they work hard, practise and are willing to challenge themselves, it is far more likely that the children will learn more, learn it faster and more thoroughly as it is embedded in their very soul – so the concepts of supposed intelligence and comparison to others does not come into play. Dweck's' assertion is that a growth mindset can be cultivated, nurtured and grown through a focus on attitudes and dispositions towards learning rather than a finished or completed product. Teachers and schools need to intentionally and explicitly praise children's effort and perseverance, thus differentiating through expectation, instead of lending more weight to learning achievements based upon a fixed outcome.

What is behaviour for learning?

Inextricably linked to developing a 'growth mindset' is the concept of 'behaviour for learning'. St. Mary's Catholic Infant School in Croydon, a truly outstanding and great school with a very diverse intake and extremely high percentage of English as an Additional Language and Pupil Premium families has, over the last three years, undertaken a rigorous review of behaviour for learning within the school. See below for Headteacher Linda O'Callaghan's observations.

Behaviour for learning

Linda O'Callaghan, Headteacher of St. Mary's Catholic Infant School, Croydon

'Behaviour for learning emphasises the crucial link between the way in which children and young people learn and their social knowledge and behaviour. Behaviour for learning focuses upon establishing positive relationships across three elements of self, others and curriculum. Good behaviour for learning at St Mary's is not about children being quiet or passive, it is about developing a positive and active involvement in the process of learning and is the product of a variety of influences:

- Relationship with self – a child who does not feel confident as a learner and who has 'internalised'* a view that they are unable to succeed as a learner will be less likely to engage in the challenge of learning and may be more inclined to present 'unwanted behaviours'.
- Relationship with others – all behaviour needs to be understood as 'behaviour in context'. Behaviour by children is triggered as much by their interactions with others (children, teachers or other adults in schools and other settings) as it is by factors internal to the child.
- Relationship with the curriculum – children's behaviour and curriculum progress are inextricably linked. Teachers who promote a sense of meaningful curriculum progress in learning for each child will be more likely to create a positive behavioural environment.

At St. Mary's our vision for learning is built upon the belief that children need to be active, confident learners. From nursery onwards, all our policies and daily classroom practice are focused on teaching our children to be independent, resilient and to view the acquisition of skills and knowledge as life-changing gifts. Our curriculum has been developed to promote independent problem solving and challenge. This should be clearly visible in every class in the way that the children will be finding the tools they need to solve a problem rather than waiting for resources to be given to them, co-operating with others in order the complete a challenge, staying on task and involved with their learning, as well as in their excitement and enthusiasm for learning new things.'

It is my contention that they internalise these conscious or sub-conscious thought patterns around the age of three or four, and the adult role in instilling these thought patterns and sense of belief is paramount – in either a positive or negative sense – hence why the requirement to have a staff team in Reception with positive growth mindsets is so vitally important so they can model this behaviour to the children. Seeing as one of the ways children learn is through imitation, they need to see and hear adults who are willing

*'Internalisation' – How does this come about, and more importantly, why? All adults have a key role in inculcating a positive self-image within the children: a 'can do' culture, a willingness to have a go and try new things out. The very youngest of children have no fear of failure or getting things wrong, they are just relentless in their pursuit of learning and knowledge, they keep going on (and often on and on!) until they have mastered a new skill such as walking or crawling and talking. They don't stop if they fail in the short term, they re-assess learnt skills and go again. It would appear that they have an innate 'growth mindset' already in place – this natural inquisitiveness and desire to find out. It appears as though it is a natural state that is dismantled through nurture – when children learn that they cannot do something, or are no good at it. How do they learn this, where do they learn this and why?

to have a go, to get things slightly wrong, to be collaborative and democratic, to laugh at themselves and to reflect. How do you do this in your classrooms everyday?

The link between Forest Schools and 'behaviour for learning'

Forest School is an innovative educational approach to outdoor play and learning and fast gaining credence in the UK. Forest Schools are not dependent on having vast tracts of woodland and can be installed by innovative practitioners in the smallest of places. In many urban schools I work with, the concept of the 'forest school' has been embraced to compensate for children's lack of opportunity to play and learn in natural playscapes and environments. The philosophy of Forest School, is to encourage and inspire individuals of any age through positive outdoor experiences.

By participating in engaging, motivating and achievable tasks and activities in a natural environment, each participant has an opportunity to develop intrinsic motivation and sound emotional and social skill – all of which form the foundations of good behaviour for learning.

Research shows that Forest Schools have demonstrated marked successes with children of all ages who visit the same local environment on a regular basis and through play, have the opportunity to learn about the natural environment, how to handle risks and most importantly to use their own initiative to solve problems and co-operate with others – in short, to develop good behaviour for learning.

At St. Mary's Infant School, although they are still in the early stages of developing a Forest School, they have already noticed rapid changes in those children's dispositions, who have until now been difficult to motivate and have been identified as passive learners. This initial anecdotal evidence is now backed with hard evidence in terms of the rapid progress through the personal and social strands of the Early Years Curriculum that a majority of these children have made, leading to improved outcomes overall and a real positive self-image on behalf of the children.

Kingfisher Community Primary School in Chatham is fortunate to have a large wooded area adjacent to the school, and the Foundation Stage team use this area on a daily basis. The children at Kingfisher, like St. Mary's, join the Reception class at levels below that which would be expected and are both fortunate to have outstanding nurseries onsite that greatly assist in narrowing the initial gaps.

Case studies from these schools reveal that children's attitudes to learning alter when in the natural environment utilising natural resources which encourage thinking skills. My definition of creativity is: 'the ability to create something out of something to represent something that is not there', which in essence is what the Reception class should be about. The case studies also reveal how children are transferring the skills and attitudes they learn in Forest School to other learning situations within the classroom. The net result is improved outcomes and a much higher percentage of children achieving a good level of development, and narrowing of the gaps in both attainment and progress.

Low independence	High independence
↓	↓
Passive children	Active children
Low challenge = high success	High challenge = low success
↓	↓
Limited learning	Unlimited learning

Figure 4. Correlation between high independence and high order thinking and challenge equating to unlimited learning potential and a growth mindset

The concept is to build upon brains through an enabling environment and positive relationships in which children have ownership of time, resources and space – as a result all children will make rapid progress and more importantly view themselves as capable and responsible learners.

This simple chart shows the correlation between high independence and high order thinking and challenge equating to unlimited learning potential and a growth mindset. Challenge here is high, as are the expectations of all stakeholders. Children might initially be less successful, but they will grow resilience and a willingness to have a go at unfamiliar activities because they can transfer knowledge and skills to these situations and take mastery of them within their own context. Conversely, if children are not coached in or given opportunities to make mistakes or try new ideas or apply knowledge to new and engaging situations, the result will be: passivity in the learning process which is adult-dominated with limited challenge yet high success precisely because activities are not challenging; low self-esteem and an unwillingness to try something different or have a go at something they are unfamiliar with – in short a closed mindset.

Question for reflection

How much independence do you truly afford the children?

Summary

Through this section we have looked at the methodology of pulling together a cohesive and agreed vision for your class, ensuring all stakeholders are an active part of the process. The role of directional and collaborative leadership has been discussed and how this influences the directionality of the classroom and all those who participate within it.

We have also looked at detailed behaviour for learning and the inculcation of growth mindsets in developing this vision further – looking at the long-term aims of not just the Reception class but the school as a whole and not just for the children and pupils but, perhaps more importantly, for the adults as well.

3 Routines and environment

'Routine' – once you have your agreed vision statement in place, one of the next tasks is to introduce a routine that supports it and to start to develop an environment that is stimulating and interesting and allows children greater autonomy in their learning and the opportunity to link learning together in meaningful contexts. Routines and environments need to be conducive to both adults and children – the environment is shared by all as a place of learning and discovery!

If I return to the analogy I made in the introduction:

> *I always think that a good Reception class should be like a favourite shop – lots of new interesting and fascinating things, a good line of solid staples and, as any excellent retailer does, a positive response to the clientele.*

If you look at your environment in this way it will free you up to think more creatively. The children are your clients, the environment is theirs not yours – your environments and routines needs to fit in with the needs and interests of the children, they should be linked with your agreed vision aims and objectives – if this happens you will have involved and engaged children taking an ownership of their environment and making progress.

Put yourself in the shoes of a four- or five-year-old in your current learning environment and look around you. Then consider these questions:

- Is the environment stimulating and interesting?
- Are there new and exciting things to explore?
- Are there cosy places to go?
- Are there appropriate resources?
- Is it culturally and developmentally appropriate?
- Are my routines supporting learning and allowing for prolonged periods of uninterrupted learning and exploration to take place?
- Do I allow enough time for children to become engaged?

- Link back to the characteristics of effective teaching and learning – can you identify active learning?
- Are there opportunities for children and adults to think creatively and critically together and plan future experiences?

Developing a routine

With your agreed vision statement in place, the next area to develop is a conducive routine that matches your aspirational and intended outcomes for the children. It should be flexible yet covering all the needs of the children, and should allow you to mediate in learning – to play, to teach new skills and knowledge and to observe. Your routine will obviously be organic and change over time, but do be aware of the notion of 'preparing' children for their next stage – treat them as they are and with what they incrementally require and the next stage will develop.

Routines in a Reception class should be flexible yet stable. This is not a dichotomy; young children do like a routine for consistencies sake, as do adults in reality. It gives them security, knowing what is going to happen every day. To this end, many schools utilise a visual timetable initially to ensure that the children are secure with the routines and expectations – this is good practice. Children are actually quite funny about routines; there have been many times when I have been in a Reception class where the routine has been altered for one reason or another and I have heard the children whispering, 'We haven't done phonics yet!' The end of the world is nigh!

Routines change throughout the year – this is part and parcel of your ongoing transition policy. As the children become more settled, as they develop the skills of independence and the attributes of persistence and resilience, so the routines will gradually alter, as will the expectations. Any initial routine needs to be developmentally and culturally appropriate – if it is not, you might be setting children up to fail at a very early stage in their school life. If your routines and expectations are not age-appropriate, and if you have members of the team who see any physical play and noise as disruptive and immature, and consequently ask children to conform to behaviours they are not physically or cognitively ready for, these seeds of under-achievement may be planted early in developing brains.

It is also worth remembering that your routines and environments will alter from year to year as new cohorts enter the classroom. All these cohorts will be at different places, will have differing needs and different make-ups – different percentages of boys and girls, SEN, EAL and PP children within them – and they will be developing at different rates, so to have a routine that is set in stone and immovable from one year to the next is just setting yourself up for a difficult and frustrating year. Be flexible and revisit your vision – you are the representations for this in the classroom.

Initial routines, based upon your assessment of observations and dialogues, focus on the utilisation of the learning space: where things are, where they go and how to access them and take care of them. It is important not to be swept along with current trends and ideals. Stick with what works well in the context of the differing needs of the children and your agreed vision. This will be enormously appreciated by your team. By all means research, read and assimilate, but ask yourself whether any radical overhauls to the routine will actually add value to the learning experiences offered to the children.

Routines must encapsulate the balance of learning supports and expectations within the Reception class. There is often a misconception as to the amount of adult-led or child-initiated learning there should be. In the days of yore, there were percentages bandied around, e.g. it became common advice that 'A good 50/50 split is what you are after in the Reception class'. This urban myth originated from somewhere, and from somebody. In hindsight this was slightly ridiculous and I believe, in many instances, mitigated against progress and lowered expectations and aspirations in many schools. There is no exact science to this – think about Goldilocks trying to getting it just right! And add to this the fact that this 'rightness' will be different year upon year. Added to this there is often a very real misconception as to what child-initiated play is, and although I am Early Years to the core, I feel that this misconception often has huge ramifications in the sometimes negative views of others regarding Reception and Foundation Stage practice.

What is child-initiated learning?

The Statutory Framework for the Early Years Foundation Stage emphasises that it is the responsibility of providers to make judgements about the mix of play and more formal teaching, as well as the balance between adult-led and child-initiated activities. The following points are taken from the Framework:

- 'Play is essential for children's development, building their confidence as they learn to explore, to think about problems, and relate to others.'

- 'Each area of learning and development must be implemented through planned, purposeful play and through a mix of adult-led and child-initiated activity.'

Between December 2014 and February 2015, Ofsted surveyed staff in 'good' or 'out-standing' early years settings. The survey explored the perceptions of teaching and play in the early years, including the perceptions of child-initiated learning, One response cited in the report, describes child-initiated activities as follows:

> 'Children choose where, when and what they want to do; it lasts as long as the activity interests and engages them.' (Teaching and play in the early years – a balancing act? Ofsted)

The same report explains:

'Ofsted does not have a preferred style or approach to teaching or play. Those working in schools and settings, rather than inspectors, are best placed to make important decisions about how children learn.'

So what does this mean in practice?

What it means is that as the Reception class teacher you will have to make this decision based upon your knowledge of where the children are placed developmentally and where they need to get to in order to show good or better progress. In reality, there are three types of learning that happen in the Reception class:

- adult-led learning – the teaching of new skills and knowledge
- independent learning – the practice of new skills
- self-initiated learning - gaining ownership of the knowledge; the child applies it, it becomes part of them.

Consequently, your routines will need to cover all these three elements of learning and they need to be explicit in the environment.

The following plan is a blue print for a day, something that you would work towards. I am very conscious and hesitant about advising practitioners in their routines as each school is different and has various complexities, but on my travels I have discovered that many

'I just let the children get on with their play. After all, it's child-initiated learning, isn't it, so I don't intervene much?'	'Proper learning only takes place with the adult. I know exactly what they are learning then and where they are.'

Too little adult focus Leads to lack of challenge. Shows misunderstanding of child initiated learning.	**Too much adult focus** Leads to lack of challenge. Shows misunderstanding of child initiated learning.

Just right
Children continuously learning in both adult-led and child-initiated activities. Adults noticing learning nuggets' and building on them, through moment to moment teaching and planned activities.

Figure 5. Adult-led learning versus child-initiated learning

schools just require a basic framework. This framework is steeped in excellent Foundation Stage practice and has the characteristics of effective teaching and learning at its core. I have used this model in a number of schools – the key thing is to take ownership of it and adapt it to suit your purposes and circumstances.

Winterbourne Infant School, a six-form entry school in Croydon, utilised this model to a great extent – the results have been an increased number of children achieving a GLD, greater adult engagement in the learning process and a serious narrowing of the gap. The main reasons behind the successes are: time allowed to be with the children; moment by moment coaching; scaffolding of learning and an understanding of roles and responsibilities on behalf of all adults.

Using the basic routine framework

How does this model run? Initially, time needs to be spent coaching the children on expectations – this is what we do here, this is how we learn.

The diagram below shows a chronological time line for the day, the numbers on the diagram relate to the different sessions and opportunities during the morning and afternoon.

Session 1

Children self-registrate and there are differentiated challenges on arrival linked to previous inputs or interests (these can stay out all day so there is no need to put anything away).

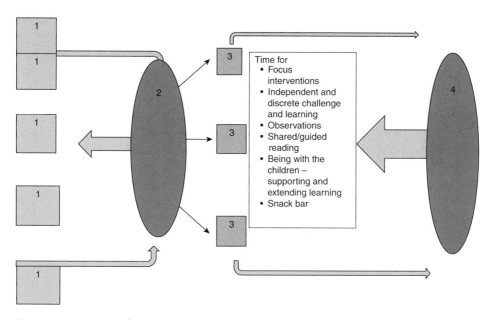

Figure 6. Basic routine framework

The children work their way through these during the course of a week. Ideally, parents or carers would be involved in this process working alongside their children – this gives the children an opportunity to apply learning across the learning areas in a meaningful context – these are not merely table-top fillers.

Session 2

If parents are in the class at this juncture, they say goodbye and the children join the adult on the carpet. (Please remember carpet times are short and sharp – the rule of thumb is age plus two minutes). After an initial 'hello and welcome' the main focus is on the learning that the children have already done. Ask open ended questions to support this, e.g. 'Did I see you? What did you discover? What learning did you use?' Obviously you will not be able to get through all the children, but this can be worked on a rota basis. The focus is on children talking about their learning and gaining confidence to talk to others. Children are naturally competitive and once you start using the language of learning others will want to join in, e.g. 'I did learning too' is a phrase often heard. This is a good time for some quick mental maths input at this time.

Session 3

I would advise that you get your phonics teaching out of the way as soon as possible so children have prolonged periods of time to apply learning in the environment. In this model there are three differentiated phonics groups (you might have more). Do utilise the Review, Teach and Practice concept, the Application of new sounds and words comes in the Independent work and challenge. The key thing here is communication between the adults as these phonics groups also act as speaking and listening and planning groups. So following the phonic input the adult introduces the challenges of the day and who might be working with whom and the children utilise talking partners to plan their learning within the environment (please refrain from using the word 'choose' – as children can 'choose' to do not a lot – focus on learning).

Session 4

During the prolonged uninterrupted learning time, children decide when to have their snack. I would suggest having an adult in the vicinity to support learning and language development. At Salfords Primary School in Redhill, the team worked a wonderful snack time with toast bar, cereal and fruit, complete with price list – children were given tokens to 'purchase' their snack, all good application of mathematical understanding. An adult was stationed in the area for a set time to support language development and key skills such as use of cutlery and cutting. Once the children have moved into Session 4, you can have a prolonged period where the adults can work with targeted groups or individuals, you can look at focused activities and interventions – what do specific children need in order to move forward? It is not a case of everybody having a go at the same activity, you will need to be more strategic than this. Children have the opportunity to get on with their learning. Observations can be carried out and adults support children in self-initiated activities. The focus at the end of the session is the learning that the children have done – recapping and supporting.

The afternoon session follows the same model, obviously without the phonics input.

This is a blue print of a very successful model – I have omitted assembly times here and other parts of the day that you might have to adhere to, such as time in the ICT suite and PE for example – but I would question the merits of these as discrete blocks of learning if they are not followed by opportunities to apply them during the day. This skeleton structure will give you a basic framework that can be adapted to suit your particular school. As the year progresses the amount of discrete 'focus' inputs might well increase. However, you must ensure that there is ample opportunity for the children to practise, revisit and apply any focus inputs into their own learning.

You will have noted that there is no 'play time' on this schematic as the children do not need one, and I would argue long into the night that this should be the case in the Infants as well. Tea breaks for staff run through the morning, just ensure ratios are met and the physical area is manageable – in many schools, the staff utilise the spill-proof thermos mugs to have their tea in, so they do not need to leave the class. Children see no difference between learning and play; the two are entwined, and I question whether playgrounds offer real opportunities for application of learning in meaningful contexts. Often, it has to be said, they do not – a slab of tarmac with some rudimentary climbing equipment does not encourage ongoing learning and application. Work that I have carried out in a number of schools concerning the delivery of the revised National Curriculum, has revealed that in the Infants, the abolishment of the 'play time' and the opportunity for greater challenge time and use of learning spaces outdoors, has led to the children gaining, over two years, an extra 64 days of learning time. As a result, progress is greater, attainment is higher, and children are far more confident in their capabilities and their ability to talk about their learning.

Your routines, as noted previously, do need to be flexible because children Reception children do tend to have the habit of getting fairly tired because their brains are generally busy problem-solving and thinking. So it is worth looking at and observing when, and where, the optimum times and places for learning are in your classrooms and when the children need to have some 'down time'. Rather like yourself, children cannot be mentally engaged all day, they and you need time to 'chill out' and do something which makes you feel secure, something that may be rudimentary but allows the brain the time to re-energize before cracking on with the next exciting learning opportunities on offer in the enabling environment you have provided. The best Reception teachers are totally aware of the rhythms of the day and consequently have differing expectations at different times of the day regarding learning – however the expectations on behaviour and respect remain constant.

As the children go through the Reception year you should, and will be adding more into the mix – shared and guided reading and writing become a non-negotiable everyday activity, as do phonics and mathematical problem-solving.

Assemblies

As a visitor to many schools, I am often confronted with the issue of assemblies. The overwhelming response to them is that they get in the way of the learning and do not allow schools to fully implement the requirements of the Foundation Stage. When you analyse it, this is true. If I am having to stop children every morning or afternoon when they might be fully engaged in the learning process, what messages am I giving to the young learners in my charge: 'Don't worry about that Amy, because where you are going and what you are going to endure are far more important to your development'. Again, I would suggest that you take yourself aside and look at the issue in an empathetic and understanding way – just because schools have always done something, it does not make it right. Often the reason for doing these activities has been lost in the mists of time and this is something that as a school, we just do. To continually break up the children's day leads to gaps in understanding and application, a lack of involvement and consequently less deep-level learning taking place. Schools continually bemoan the quantity of knowledge they need to impart during an academic year, yet too often established routines get in the way of allowing children the time to practise and apply all this knowledge. Just think – time, time and more time.

If we just question why have assemblies – what are the children getting out of them? Arguments of community usually abound here; making the children feel part and parcel of the school. But this can be done gradually. What is most important to the children in your class is the immediate here and now; this is where the learning is, this is where the experiences are that will have greatest immediate impact on their long-term development and learning. Celebration assemblies are a good and positive thing, so long as they are culturally and developmentally appropriate and can bring a definite sense of community to the school with parents and carers being included.

Snack bars

Snack bars, or fruit time, is a fascinating part of the day and each school has different ways of implementing this. Some use the more free-flow model whereby children decide when to have a snack as part of their learning day, others are more prosaic and result in everybody stopping what they are doing to sit in a big circle. The latter is often justified as a speaking and listening opportunity or for PSE development.

As an aside, I would question the logic and wisdom of giving children citrus fruit, complete with natural sugars, to eat alongside milk to drink– an interesting combination to be sitting on top of a young stomach!

I would suggest that you offer the children a rich array of snacks, things which are of nutritional value and give the young brains the energy they require to keep on functioning at a high level. Best practice models I have noted and supported are built around an open snack time policy – which is directly attributable to the schools vision for the children in the Foundation Stage, notably in developing independence and persistence. Snack bars in many schools are open for a limited amount of time during the morning session, and sometimes in the afternoon. Available for the children are healthy cereals and toast. An adult is located in the snack zone as a model for speaking and listening and for practising the use of utensils for cutting pouring and for sharing. The levels and complexity of the conversations I have overheard in these open snack bars are remarkable.

There are unlimited opportunities to use these times for focusing on certain aspects with identified children or just having the joy of talking and listening with young and enquiring minds, finding out all sorts of information about them and their experiences that will assist in planning further meaningful learning opportunities. If I was to offer any advice here, I would suggest a more open model. Initially it is tricky to implement, and there needs to be agreed values around the snack bar in terms of sitting and eating (I cannot abide seeing children wandering about the environment eating – but maybe that is just me) and using the correct utensils, listening to each other and being respectful – this is inculcating skills for life.

How do I know that a Reception class is good or better? The answer is simple. Children treat things and each other with respect and they put lids on pens without being asked or reminded to do so – this is autonomy in action.

Developing learning environments that are fit for purpose

It is not always a matter of ordering copious expensive resources – look at the affordability. What do your resources afford children in terms of long-term learning and how affordable are they? To be honest, the best resources are usually those of an open-ended nature that allow children to be creative and imaginative. To quote Margaret McMillan: 'The best kept classroom and the richest cupboard is roofed only by the sky'.

It does seem, in this modern age of acadamisation, that the outdoor space in particular is used as a selling point for the school with lots of impressive-looking expensive equipment – which when analysed do not offer the children long-term learning opportunities. The types of resources you should be sourcing are those that can be utilised for a multitude of endeavors and in different ways. To revisit my definition of creativity (see Chapter 2, page 31), real creativity is 'the ability to create something out of something to represent something that is not there' – that is high-level thinking and young children do this all the time.

Setting out your physical environment is key, and depending on the space you have available you might have to compromise or extend. It is not really necessary to have areas for all 17 areas of learning, although I do see this often – big notices proudly announcing for example 'the maths area' but with no children in the zone as they are working elsewhere. One would question the purpose of these discrete zones. Learning, for young children happens everywhere and at all times – maths will not only happen, if it does at all, in the 'maths area'. It will happen in the sand, the water, the construction and the role play areas. The key is to allow children the autonomy to make links in their learning by using literacy and numeracy skills throughout the enabling environment.

The environment plays a key role in supporting and extending children's development and learning. Enabling environments that encourage children to play because they feel relaxed, comfortable and 'at home' in them. When children feel emotionally safe and secure they are able to explore and find out about the place they are in and the things they can see, touch, manoeuvre or manipulate. In the previous EYFS framework, the environment was described in terms of three aspects:

- the emotional environment
- the outdoor environment
- the indoor environment.

These three aspects are still highly relevant today (despite no longer being mentioned in the revised framework). Together, they make up the environment for play and learning in Reception.

The emotional environment

The learning environment is more than the physical space because it contains the emotions of the children who spend time in it, the staff that work there and the parents who leave their children there. The emotional environment is an invisible measure of 'feelings' – sometimes it can have a 'feel-good' factor where the children, staff and parents feel positive, and at others it can have a 'not so good' feel about it when children, staff or parents are down or unhappy. Maintaining positive feelings is important for staff, children and parents, but equally important is that if children feel safe in the emotional environment, they can express their feelings safely, knowing that their parents or staff are nearby to help them if they feel overwhelmed by these. Teaching children ways to talk about and express their feelings allows them to externalise them safely, rather than to cover them up and leave them hidden away. Feelings that are expressed in safety, are far easier to deal with than those which are left unresolved.

With regard to this, I refer you back to the judgements that Ofsted make with regard to personal development, behaviour and welfare (see Chapter 1, page 15) and in particular children's:

- 'sense of achievement and commitment to learning through a positive culture that is evident across the whole setting

- self-confidence, self-awareness and understanding of how to be a successful learner
- enjoyment of learning and the development of their independence and ability to explore their surroundings and use their imagination
- emotional security, through emotional attachments with practitioners and carers, and their physical and emotional health.'

Emotional well-being and security are key for learning. If children are emotionally secure in their routines and environments, they will have a far more positive approach to learning and be more open to a growth mindset, this is because the situation meets their basic needs, they have a positive self-concept, they are in touch with themselves and are starting to understand the needs and requirements of others and regulate themselves accordingly. The result is emotional health. This emotional security permits deep level learning to take place. We shall return to this concept later in the book when we discuss in greater detail the leadership of a team and ensuring that the team's emotional well-being is being addressed (see Chapter 7, page 105).

The outdoor environment

Children gain enormous benefits from learning outdoors. Ideally they should have access to outdoor space on a daily basis, regardless of weather – there is no such thing as bad weather, just bad clothing! Being outdoors allows children to move around without many of the restrictions of being inside. They can fill their lungs with clean air and use all of their senses to appreciate the colours, noises, and the sense of space and of scale. Being outdoors builds confidence and allows opportunities for big scale play, problem-solving and creativity in the company of other children. Physical activity is enhanced. So is calculated risk-taking. In the outdoors, research shows that children's use of language is five times greater than indoors. Endorphins are released in the brain which relax the children and assist in prolonging the feel good factor. (Stephanie Phillipa Kennedy: 'Freedom for speech: outdoor play and its potential for young children's conceptual, linguistic and communicative development')

Whilst it is true that not all children like the outdoors, positive adult encouragement to utilise the space can often mitigate against a child's reluctance. Resources don't need to be expensive: old tyres, some logs and crates will stimulate imagination and can be used in a number of ways, for example: a sheet can become a den; flower pots and hanging baskets and a 'wild area' give contact with the natural world. The outdoors supports active learning and when balanced with quiet areas for reflection can really enhance children's development.

Outdoors can sometimes be problematic due to space – sometimes the space is too large to be manageable and as a result adults spend their time 'policing' the play rather than interacting with it and extending it. Conversely, sometimes the outdoor area is small and practitioners worry about the coverage of all the learning aspects.

Photo 4. Quick and easy tyre climbing frame: St. Mary's Infant School

Photo 5. Home-made fire engine: St. Mary's Infant School

Photo 6. Boys' reading and writing zone: St. Mary's Infant School

The indoor environment

Indoor space needs careful planning as it needs to be flexible to accommodate children's changing interests and needs. Resources should be of the highest quality. Books need to be attractive and well-maintained and reflect children's fascinations. Resources such as blocks for building with, felt pens, chalks or pencils for mark making, clothes for dressing up in and small items such as cars, dolls and jigsaws should be easily accessible for children.

Areas you MUST include:

- Cosy and comfortable book corners – do ensure that books permeate all areas – ensure that you have high quality reading texts. If the children leave the Reception classes knowing at least 20 key texts off by heart and back to front, you as a practitioner will have done a phenomenal job because the children will have secure knowledge of narrative and how a story works. This will allow them to innovate these stories in order to create their own narratives (see recommended book list overleaf). I am also a great believer in having proper grown-up sized sofas in the book zones, as these are comfortable and allow children and adults to snuggle in for quality reading times.

- Role play areas – indoors and out. Bear in mind that at Reception age children often choose gender specific activities through role play, so it is fine to have different role plays in your environment to meet the various needs of your young learners. There is much research at the moment into the 'genderification' of the classroom. Ensure that your environment is enabling for both boys and girls so there are fascination traps for both, and also ensure that your staff team see the learning in the activity and not just the behaviour.

- Construction and creative areas

- Writing opportunities throughout

- Signage and key prompts for question streams to support adults

- Displays that reflect learning – including children having ownership of what goes on the display, e.g. 'I am proud of this because...' Also include the 'wow' moments from home to strengthen the home–school link. St. Peter's C of E Primary School in Farnham have perhaps the most wonderful 'wow' moments from home, and these act as a fantastic display in the entrance foyer – this will be discussed in the chapter regarding progress and assessment (see Chapter 5, page 81).

Look at each area and ensure that there are opportunities for mathematical thinking and application – please have number lines and 100 squares out and about in the environment.

Role play outdoors can sometimes be problematic. A good way to get over any issues is to zone off the outside area into different learning bays complete with resources that

Photo 7. Using a picket fence to break up outdoor space: Send C of E First School, Woking

the children can access independently – storage trolleys are excellent here. Send C of E First School in Woking, have used picket fencing to break up the outdoor space – it also supports developing children's play for they get into role as they go into a zone. Often adults have the unenviable task of setting up the outdoor area (I would suggest that once you have zoned off a specific area, you allow children to help you with this) – they decide on what they want and where, the key point is that on completion they also put it back to its rightful place.

It is important not to view the indoors and outdoors as two separate entities – they are not, they are one emotional learning space and need to be viewed as a coherent whole, but often due to the complexities and restraints faced when putting together a rich learning environment, it might be easier to work on either the outdoors or indoors individually first and then pull them together as a whole – otherwise you might get lost in the process and the whole does not equal the sum of the parts.

Suggested book list

In my opinion, *all* these quality books should be included in your Reception class – non-negotiable!

Julia Donaldson: *The Gruffalo*; *The Gruffalo's Child*; *The snail and the whale*; *Room on the Broom*; *The Smartest Giant in Town*

The Little Red Hen

Michael Rosen: *We're Going on a Bear Hunt*

David McKee: *Not now, Bernard*; *Elmer* series

Jill Murphy: all publications

Jez Alborough: all publications

Shirley Hughes: *Alfie* series

Valerie Thomas: *Winnie the Witch* series

Martin Waddell: *Owl Babies*; *The Pig in the Pond*; *Farmer Duck*; The *Little Bear Stories*

John Prater: *Once Upon a Time*

Maurice Sendak: *Where the Wild Things Are*

Trish Cooke and Helen Oxenbury: *So Much!*

Eric Carle: *The Bad-tempered Ladybird*; *The Very Hungry Caterpillar*

Mini Grey: *Traction Man* series

Lynley Doss: *Hairy Maclairy* series

Eileen Browne: *Handa's Surprise*; *Handa's Hen*

Niki Daly: *Jamela's Dress*

Penny Dale: *Ten in the Bed*

Sarah Hayes – *This is the Bear* series

Judith Kerr: *The Tiger Who Came to Tea*; *Mog* series

Janet and Allan Ahlberg: *Funnybones*

Allan Ahlberg: *The Gaskitt* stories

Simon Prescott - *On a Dark Dark Night*

David Roberts: *Dirty Bertie*

Werner Holzwarth: *The Story of the Little Mole who Knew it was None of his Business*

Aidan Potts; *Uneversaurus*

Claire Freedman; *Alien's love Underpants*

Colin McNaughton: *Who's Been Sleeping in my Porridge?*

Jill Bennett: *Noisy poems*

Summary

During this chapter we have looked at the importance of having conducive and agreeable routines that will afford the children **time** to become involved in learning and allow the adults to undertake focused precision inputs to mediate and scaffold children's independent learning. We have also looked in detail at the learning environments, indoors and out with a view to ensuring that it is seen as a coherent and conjoined learning **space** that offers exciting and meaningful opportunities for children to apply learning.

The two key things to focus on are:

1. Space

The space available in different classrooms will vary. Although availability of space is certainly an issue, teachers can frequently make this even more challenging by not making the best use of what is available. An untidy, cluttered environment, full of things kept 'just in case they come in useful one day', limits children's ability to move around and restricts their freedom to play and explore. This in turn can often lead to problems with behaviour as children become frustrated or bored. A high-quality environment for young children should:

- be clean, tidy and uncluttered
- be used flexibly by practitioners throughout the day in response to children's moods and interests

- include cosy, quiet spaces where children can play quietly, look at books, rest, or sleep
- contain only the furniture that is absolutely essential, leaving plenty of free floor space for children's play
- have space for individual activities and for group interaction
- be resourced with interesting open-ended toys and resources to look at, touch and explore
- support and enhance the play opportunities of all children
- have resources stored at a height where children can see and access them
- create interesting environments to explore.

2. Time

As well as creating a physical space that is attractive and full of interesting resources, it is important to think carefully about how you manage the time that is spent in it. Children need time to become absorbed in what they are doing, often repeating things again and again until their curiosity is satisfied. They need time to play on their own, time to play with friends, and time to be part of a larger group at story time or when dancing or making music. Children in the Reception classes will enjoy being involved in projects and activities that extend over several days, providing the opportunity to come back to things and explore them in greater depth. A flexible approach to time management which takes account of the needs and interests of the children, rather than a fixed routine which must be followed minute by minute, will lead to better outcomes for everyone. This approach gives children the opportunity to concentrate for long periods of time, investigating resources and exploring situations that interest them, thereby demonstrating deep involvement and high-level learning. Experience shows that this approach leads to a calmer atmosphere in the classroom, gives more time for children to become engrossed in what they are doing, and results in an increase in emotional well-being, regulation and self-control.

If you get these aspects right, and it will take time to plan, embed and review your routines and environments, you will have far greater ownership of your teaching – you will be able to talk with professionalism and confidence about what you do, why you do it, and most importantly, the impact it has on the outcomes for children.

4 Observation, assessment and planning

'Planning' – it's the bane of many teachers' lives. What do we plan? How do we plan? What do we plan from? If you are not careful, planning can take over your practice. Often there are unrealistic expectations on behalf of the senior leadership who require all the planning to be typed up and on their desk every Monday morning. Remember that you cannot plan effectively if you do not have in place an effective and manageable observation and assessment system. The cycle starts with observations – what are the children doing, where and how? Assessment of these observations is crucial – what are they telling you about individual children? Once you have assessed your observations then the planning process can start. Too often teachers plan first and try to fit children into the plan. This will result in a delivered adult-led curriculum that does not meet the needs of the children and exasperation and exhaustion on behalf of the adults.

A plan is what it says – 'a plan'. It is not set in stone and should be a moveable and adaptable feast. It is important that you gain ownership of this otherwise you will be guided by others who do not know your children or how they work and learn. In reality, you cannot plan for a Friday on a Monday – how do you know where the learning will go through the week – is should be based upon your observations and assessments of the children. To follow a model of rigidity in planning will often lead to *activity-based*, not *learning-based* planning and provision. The most exciting, and perhaps daunting, aspect of Early Years is the freedom to respond to what you see the children doing and adapt your planning and provision to suit.

Observing to inform planning

There are numerous types of observation – but remember the EYFS framework does state the following:

'Practitioners must consider the individual needs, interests, and stage of development of each child in their care, and must use this information to plan a challenging and enjoyable experience for each child in all of the areas of learning and development.'

'Practitioners should respond to their own day-to-day observations about children's progress and observations.'

'Assessment should not entail prolonged breaks from interaction with children, nor require excessive paperwork. Paperwork should be limited to that which is absolutely necessary to promote children's successful learning and development.'

(*Statutory Framework for the Early Years*, DfE)

To me, what this is pointing towards is short-term observations, ensuring that all the children are observed on a regular basis – some of these might be a longer observation, a photo, and an anecdote of something jotted down. An observation needs to be of a 'WOW' moment, something that is significant to an individual. Look at an observation as something that surprises and delights you – something that you did not know about a child.

Observations are not a tick list nor a checklist of statements from the *Development Matters* documentation (see below). There is and never was an expectation on the quantity of observations – it is and always has been about the quality of them.

Development Matters in the Early Years Foundation Stage (EYFS)

This document, published by Early Education is important guidance; the document highlights the skills, knowledge and attributes children should be displaying at certain ages. The statements are not hierarchical and should not be used as learning objectives.

Your role as a Reception teacher is far more forensic and consequently interesting than that. You should have in-depth knowledge of the statements from the documentation, as you should have in-depth understanding of child development. The statements are there to guide you. The question you should be asking is: 'Are the children displaying skills and knowledge equivalent to the age band?'. If the answer is yes, then the thoughts should be how to extend and consolidate the learning. If the answer is no, the documentation can be used to gauge where developmentally they might be.

Too often overlooked in the *Development Matters* documentation are the tables on positive relationships and enabling environments. To my mind, these are far more important than the development statements themselves, as they give teachers and practitioners guidance as to what they should be providing in terms of the environment and routines which are *developmentally* appropriate.

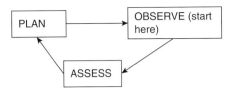

Figure 7. Development Matters in the Early Years Foundation Stage (EYFS)

Observation and planning system

The *Development Matters* document stresses the importance of starting the planning process with observation:

Observe

- What are the children doing, where and with whom?
- What are their fascinations and interests?

Assess

Assess the observations as a team.

- What are they telling you about the children as unique individuals?
- What Characteristics of Effective Learning are they displaying?
- Where might they be sitting within the development bands?

Plan

Plan inputs, provision and support based upon your assessment and analysis of your observations – you must include your whole team' in this process. Then start the cycle again.

What is observation?

- Watching
- Listening
- Noticing what children are doing as a whole – their personality, behaviour, what they say, and their learning
- Noticing how they respond to your setting, to different approaches, to different people
- Noticing how they respond to new experiences, signs of how they are feeling.

Types of observation

There are many sorts of observation. Some might be a longer narrative description of learning and interactions that are taking place, others might be shorter, capturing a moment of excitement. The key is that it does not matter what type of observation you use, but it must add value, tell you something that you might not know and inform your future provision. Observations are not an end in themselves. During my travels, the issue of observation is a continued problematic area. The point is that you, as the class teacher, will have to take ownership of any system and make it work for you. There is nothing more disheartening than seeing practitioners taking copious observations and then not knowing what to do with them.

Any observation should tell you something about the child, but it also must be remembered that your provision and how children are responding to it, their independence and responsibility are sometimes the intangible parts that are very difficult to observe. This is not a problem; this is in effect good practice, because the environment, expectations and routines are meeting the needs of the children and consequently what you are seeing is what they do every day – so I would ask would you need to write an observation on it? How the children respond to the learning environment in everyday contexts is in fact an on-going observation and reflection of your provision.

Next steps and observations is an area that often teachers and practitioners tie themselves up in knots over. Does there need to be a 'next step' for each observation? You will have to ask if this is manageable and practical. The chances are that this is a very laudable principle, but is not practical. It of course is dependent on what the observation is saying.

Immediate responses to observations should be explicit on your on-going provision planning – we have noted this today, so tomorrow we are going to provide . . . Ideally, and I would suggest that this becomes part of your practice, observations and knowledge of the children will be assessed regularly and any 'next steps' will follow from this rigorous assessment of the complete knowledge the team has of children in the class. So in short, every observation cannot practically have a next step. Observations are building up a picture of the whole child and assessment of these will allow you to develop the whole child and focus on barriers to learning rather than look at specific details which invariably centre around the numeracy and literacy elements – as if these hold more weight than the other aspects of learning and developing.

Why observe?

We gather essential information about the children:

- their individuality
- their stage of development

- their interests

- their needs

- their learning styles

- to share with parents

- to give us an insight into the received curriculum, thereby challenging assumption.

Ensure that the approach to planning and observation you promote starts with observation of the children, clearly adds value to the provision for the children and is not an end in itself.

It is imperative that all members of the team are involved in the observation process, as children will respond differently to each adult, and adults will pick up on different aspects of learning. The system that I would suggest, starts by putting together a rota system so a number of children each day are the focus of the observations. You will not be stalking these children with a clipboard or the iPad, but all your team will be aware of who they are. If your routines are now in place they should be giving you ample time to be with the children, playing, exploring and observing. Such a system will ensure that over a two-week period all your children have been observed at self-initiated or adult-initiated challenges.

Week 1

Monday	Tuesday	Wednesday	Thursday	Friday
John	Mohammed	Porsche	Indira	Bert
Ismael	Shaheen	Mercedes	Harry	Ernie
Billy	April	Mondeo	Alfie	Kermit

Week 2

Monday	Tuesday	Wednesday	Thursday	Friday
Sharon	Sophie	Michael	Chantelle	Iqbal
June	Jack	Linda	Barry	Harry
Mandy	Patricia	Sarah	Trevor	Noreen

Figure 8. The rolling rota of observation

Put any observations and evidence straight into children's records *so there is no taking records home during the weekends – get the bureaucracy out of the way quickly. If you are using an electronic system get the observations and photos sent to the relevant files.*

The best models I have noted involve all practitioners, and time has been set aside after the working day to meet for a maximum of 15 minutes to discuss what was going on during the day – this might entail some discussion on your behalf with senior leadership as hours for staff can be different. But, and I strongly argue this case, the point of school is for assisting developing children and consequently hard decisions need to be made around working hours and expectations on the adults who are supporting this development. At these short meetings, conversations then will centre on who was doing what and where, and how this can be extended the following day. This leads to reflective practice. A simple format is useful that is minuted daily and acts as evidence of the reflective practitioner.

What did you see?	Where was the learning?	Possible extensions	Adult responsible for supporting learning
Bert and Ernie in the role play – playing in role as a shopkeeper and customer	Mathematical language of bigger and smaller. Weighing objects and adding and subtracting numbers up to 10	Include price lists – opportunities for children to write numbers. Pricing up of shop goods – introduce money to the role play	Neil to support language development and note how children solve practical problems

Figure 9. Reflective observation

This in effect is short-term planning – based upon what you have noted and how you and the team are going to extend the learning opportunities. It is useful and practical to also keep a checklist of observations to ensure that you are getting coverage and that children have access to all areas of learning. This will also allow you to look at your provision and ask questions about where the learning is happening and which areas are being covered, and which areas are less so – where do you need to intervene? Hale School in Farnham have perfected this model and the impact on raising outcomes for children is amazing, children are also given opportunities to return to their interests over a number of days – this reflective planning has enabled all adults to become decision makers in the classroom based upon how the children are responding to the opportunities provided. This democratic model also allows the children to become part of the planning process.

Learning detectives

I first encountered 'learning detectives' at Littleton Church of England Infant School in Shepperton. Headteacher Rachel Barton is a passionate and excellent exponent of the development of growth mindsets throughout the school. The focus at the school is on building up the confidence and vocabulary within the children to talk about learning and also to understand what learning entails, so within this the school is introducing positive behaviour for learning. Planning at Littleton always starts with an 'enquiry question'. I shall return to this fantastic approach during the section on planning (page 72).

Name	John	Ismael	Billy	Chantelle	Sarah
Speaking	**	*	*	*	**
Listening and attention	*	**	*	*	**
Understanding	**	**	*	*	**
Moving and handling	*	***	**	**	****
Health and self-care	*	*		*	*
Self-confidence and self-awareness				*	*
Managing feelings and behaviour	*	**	*		**
Making relationships		*	*	*	**
Reading	**	*	*	**	**
Writing	**	*		**	**
Numbers	***	*	*	**	**
Shape, space and measures	*	**	*	*	*
People and communities	**	*	**	***	**
Understanding the world	**		*	**	
Technology	*	**	*	*	**
Exploring and using media and materials	**	*	**	*	**
Being Imaginative	*	**	*	**	*

Figure 10. Checklist of observations

I have borrowed the 'learning detective' concept from Littleton and have developed it further with schools I support to ensure that it not only focuses on the learning but also becomes part and parcel of your observational system. As noted previously, if you focus on three children a day for your observational schedule, your 'observational' children are the learning detectives for the day.

What is a learning detective? *Put basically, these are your eyes and ears on the classroom floor, they detect the learning that is taking place – who is doing 'good' learning and why.*

'Staff provide a good range of stimulating, interesting activities that motivate and engage children. Children enjoy all that they do and particularly enjoy being 'learning detectives' and questioning each other about what they know.' (Ofsted report: Kingfisher Primary School, Chatham)

It is important to note that you and your team do not ignore all the other wonderful learning happening in the classroom, you would not say, 'George, I love your tower and can see you have worked incredibly hard thinking about it, but can you do it on Wednesday when I am observing you'. Of course you would take an observation of this significant moment in George's learning, but your and your team's focus would be on the detectives for the day, not, I stress following them about, but everybody being aware of who they are.

It is a good idea to make some sheriff badges or something similar for them to wear so everybody can recognise them. The children do love it, and from a visitor's perspective there is nothing more brilliant than when you ask a detective what the badge represents and they are able to vocalise their responsibility for the day – it is empowering. It is a meaningful game you play with the children – on the one hand you are asking them to look for learning and positive learning behaviours in the environment, and on the other you are noting their learning and learning behaviours.

At the end of the session, the learning detectives come to the front and, with sensitive adult support:

1   talk about the learning they have seen others undertaking and why it might be 'good' learning

2   talk about the learning they have done.

This is reinforced by the adult using prompt questions so the children are reflecting on their own work, e.g.

- What went well?
- What was tricky?
- How can we make it even better?

The other children in the class join in the conversation offering ideas and support. If you have interactive whiteboards display photos as prompts, or use the visualizer for any written work. This is PSED and the Characteristics of Effective Learning in action.

I saw a lovely example of this at The Grange Community Infant School in Addlestone. One of the challenges was to make a rocket for a teddy to go to the moon in. One little boy talked openly about how he and his friends did it, what they used, the skills they implemented and how he felt about the processes. When asked what was tricky, he replied that the group could not work the sticky tape properly, 'It gets all tangled' he said. But he said that they 'kept trying and worked together to sort it out, one of us would pull it out and somebody else did the cutting.' The teacher then asked the children if anybody else found the sticky tape tricky. To which there was an overwhelming response that they all did. 'Ah,' said the teacher, 'I'll have to teach you that tomorrow, won't I?'

This is just excellent reflective planning. In order to gain independence and autonomy the children needed to be taught the skill of the tape dispenser. This wasn't on the plan, but due to the reflective nature of practice, it was added in.

I would suggest making a display out of the learning detective initiative, so any visitor to your classroom can see the reflective learning that is occurring on a daily basis and how the children are an integral part of the process.

The display below from Salfords Primary School in Redhill is an excellent example of the reflective practice. Children's voices are clear and loud in the environment – vocalising their learning and the learning of others – it is truly outstanding practice.

Smitham Primary School in Coulsdon treat the learning detectives with great respect, and when it is time for feedback the theme tune for *Mission Impossible* is played to add excitement and meaning to the exercise. As you can imagine, the children adore it and look forward to the sessions with great enthusiasm.

In many schools that I work with, this learning detective concept has been taken into the years following Reception class and the detectives are in action throughout the school – reflecting on the good learning, what has been learnt, how learning took place and the next steps in the learning journey. Consequently, within these schools, the expectations that are introduced and scaffolded in the Reception classes are further embedded and developed in subsequent year groups. There is commonality of language within the school and shared expectations in each year group that builds upon what has gone on previously and adds extra value.

Photo 8. Learning detectives display: Salfords Primary School, Redhill

Planning

Once the observations and schedules are in place, the assessment process takes place. Initially this would be on a formative basis, utilising the information the observations are providing, assessing them, what they are telling you and then move into the planning phase. Deeper level assessment as to children's level of development would take place at regular, minimum half termly intervals, to inform strategic precision teaching and intervention.

Key questions to ask when planning

- Developmentally where are the children when they arrive in the setting?
- What do my observations tell me about children's progress?
- Are all children making good progress relative to their starting points?
- Are there particular children whose progress we should be looking at in closer detail?
- Who are our vulnerable groups?
- Is there an area of learning we want to track?
- Do we cover all areas of learning equally well?
- Do we need to look at an area of provision in order to extend it?
- Is my current system of planning fit for purpose?

On entry assessment

As from September 2016 it will become a requirement for schools to undertake an approved base line assessment for children joining the Reception class. As an independent adviser, I find this whole concept slightly absurd. The vast majority of schools have been doing 'on entry' observations and assessments for years, based upon a solid observational system and an understanding of child development. These observations would be carried out within a couple of weeks to give an overview of where individuals and groups are sitting against the *Development Matters* bands – subsequent developmentally-appropriate provision would be implemented to meet the needs of the children and ensure that progress will be accelerated.

What irks me is the lack of trust in teachers' professional judgements, it is as if the Department for Education are saying your knowledge and professionalism accounts for nothing and instead you are going to have to follow a prosaic model that can take up until half term in the Autumn to complete – by which time the children will have learnt a fair amount. So will the 'on entry' judgement be an accurate assessment? Schools will be missing a half term of teaching opportunities.

One particular model suggests that you undertake observations when a child is fully involved. This is odd, because you will have had to observe a child to find out what they do, what they like and where they are most emotionally-settled in order to provide opportunities for them to become fully involved and settled – so in essence 'on entry' observation has already been completed when you have found out this initial information. The use of involvement levels should be used as a method of quality assurance and I shall return to this during the section on leading and developing the Reception team (see Chapter 7, pagde 105).

My findings from the trials of on entry have revealed that schools have completed their on entry judgements but have also kept initial observations as the real starting point for their children. Where this will all lead I am not sure, but my main concern is the lack of respect given to teachers in their ability to properly assess and plan for the children in their charge.

Once you have collated and collected observations on your children, initially from on entry and then on a regular basis, it is now time to analyse them – what do they tell you about individuals or groups of children? The use of the following schematic will assist with your future planning.

What do children need to be taught according to their level of ability?	What can they discover by themselves?
When and how will I observe what children have learnt?	Where and when can they practise/ consolidate what they have learnt?

Figure 11. Key questions to ask of observations and planning for provision

Developing learning heroes and reflective practice

The School inspection handbook states that

'Inspectors will consider:

- how well teaching nurtures, engages and motivates children and promotes their sense of achievement and the commitment to learning

- children's enjoyment of learning, including their participation and willingness to make choices and decisions, and the extent to which children are active and inquisitive learners who are creative and think critically'

This is encouraging as these statements focus on the key aspects of the Foundation Stage and in particular behaviour for learning as encapsulated in the Characteristics of Effective Learning. Behaviour for learning is currently high on the agenda. I introduced it as a concept in Chapter 2 (page 31), but here we move on to putting the ideals into a practical context in everyday practice.

To introduce and support behaviour for learning it is vital that all staff use the language of learning throughout the day, and there is expectation on behalf of leadership of the language that adults use. I have a real issue with the term 'choose' – I do get slightly irritated when I hear practitioners asking children to 'choose what to do'. Well the very looseness of the term precludes learning, for children can 'choose' to do not a lot, to wander about all day, to lie down under a table. The key is to set the children off on 'learning', e.g. by asking, 'Where are you going to do your learning today?' This is a good introduction to getting the language out in the popular domain. Once the children have become confident with this language of learning, the fun stuff can start to happen and the thinking becomes deeper and more reflective. The children will gradually see themselves and others as an active part of the learning processes in the classroom and within the school. This is because the focus shifts from the 'what' you are going to learn to the 'how' you are going to do this.

All of this goes right back to your shared vision and values – the nature of learners you wish to develop, not only in the Reception class, for this cannot be done in isolation, but throughout the entire school.

What is a learning hero?

A learning hero is a character, or set of characteristics and interests that the children can identify with. They stem from your expected outcomes for the children, in terms of their wider personal and social development and well-being. They extol agreed values of how the children work together in the classroom.

At Kingfisher Primary School in Chatham, the learning heroes for this year have taken the form of dinosaurs because the children had a huge fascination in dinosaurs. The staff, in a very creative way, took this interest and formulated with the children a series of characters that encapsulate how learning happens in the classrooms.

This display is prominently positioned within the classroom and these characters and their attributes can be found all around the learning environment, both indoors and out.

St. James C of E Primary School in Weybridge have also embraced the learning heroes model and have turned to popular books as their 'heroes', looking to develop eight elements.

I particularly enjoy this model because it is based on literature and the discussions with the children not only centre on what might be happening in the story, but at a deeper level developing an innate understanding of subtext, empathy and morality within the stories – all pretty deep stuff for five-year-olds, but just how exciting is it?

St. Mary's Catholic Infant School in Croydon have also created their own learning hero characters to support learning. Their characters were based upon the key attributes of what makes a good learner, agreed by all stakeholders through the vision statement journey. They looked in particular at persistence, resilience, creativity, independence and problem-solving – key skills for life in school and more importantly life after school and into

Shareonyx – I **share** my ideas and resources

Explorosaur – I **explore** everything around me

Solveosaurus Rex – I work hard to **solve problems**

Tryatops – I try my best and **never give up**

Thinkadocus – I **think carefully** about what I learn

Stickasaurus – I stick at tasks and **persevere**

Askaraptor – I **ask questions** and find things out

Photo 9. Learning heroes display: Kingfisher Primary School, Chatham

I **pretend and play** like Elmer

I **explore** like the family in Bear Hunt

I **try** new things like the Very Hungry Caterpillar

I am **proud** of my achievements like the Smartest Giant

I **think** of my own ideas like the Snail and the Whale

I find ways to **solve problems** like Superworm

I am **curious** like Percy the Park Keeper

I **keep going** when things get tough like Mrs Large

I **choose new ways** of doing things like Lola

Photo 10. Learning heroes display: St. James' C of E Primary School, Weybridge

adulthood – focusing very much on the bigger picture of why the school is there and what it is trying to achieve in the long term.

Schools such as these are great schools because they are not driven by outside influences and changes in legislation or documentation, but rather by the needs of the children and families in their communities, ensuring that at the centre of practice is the desire for all children to do well and achieve the best that they can.

These are just three examples of some of the outstanding work I have encountered and supported in many schools, and the similarities in all these schools is that the focus is very much on developing the language and behaviour of learning, sharing with the children in child-friendly ways what constitutes a good learner and the good behaviour that runs alongside everything that both adults and children do in the school. Behaviour for learning is an integral part of the Inspection process and cuts to the nub of what schooling is about, it is the link between the delivered and received curriculum and how children are an active participant in the process. It is about willingness to 'have a go', to extend, to think and to reason. It is inextricably linked with the development of growth mindsets and it is imperative that all members of staff model this behaviour and language. The best practice that I have witnessed is when children are displaying autonomy in the classroom, they know the requirements and the expectations and are able to follow and vocalise them with increasing confidence.

So how does all this fit together? It is simple. Any discussion or feedback plenary with the children brings the conversation back to the central tenets: 'Where are you going to do your learning and how are you going to do it'. This sort of dialogue pulls out the language of thinking and encourages open-ended questioning and possibility thinking for both adults and children and consequently higher order thinking and reasoning takes place. It also encourages all stakeholders to 'have a go' at something because everything is possible – it might just need some deeper thinking, consultation and refinement.

Curriculum mapping

Planning formats are a constant worry for many teachers. There is a lack of consistency as to the levels of planning that are required, and no guidelines. As a result, many schools get driven by their planning and the formats that might be obligatory for individual schools. The reasons for this have probably been lost in time, no one can remember why they are doing such a copious amount of paperwork, and the whole system and culture has become one of: 'Because we have always done this'.

Let's just put the handbrake on for a while and think about why we do what we do, and who the planning is actually for. If it is not for the children in the class, then, to be honest it is pretty pointless. And please remember that we are talking about four- and five-year-old children here – most of our time should be spent with them rather than locked away planning.

Your vision statement is in reality your long-term aim, and some kind souls have already written the Foundation Stage curriculum as it is, so why would you try and re-invent the wheel? I do think it very pertinent to work with your Reception team – and if you are fortunate to have a nursery on site, the nursery and your Year 1 colleagues – to devise an aspiration, skills and development map across the three years, so each preceding year can see the expectations and milestones at the end of the year and consequently support children to reach this level. In many schools, this collegiate way of working is commonplace across all phases of school life. It is worth focusing on basic skills here, rather than trying to cover all the areas of learning – get the aspirations in basic skills right and the other areas of learning will, and do, fall into place.

The curriculum mapping example in Appendix 1 (page 125) shows development across the Foundation Stage in the basic skills areas. It is not a definitive document and you might like to use it as a starting point – adding to it aspirations for Year 1, but this will need careful consideration to ensure that the progression and aspiration is equal in each Year group and takes into account the new milestones and expectations of the revised National Curriculum. What this also assists with is the agreeing of a sound and responsible pedagogic approach and also assisting teachers to see where the children have come from, where they are going and to diagnose any gaps in understanding. Curriculum mapping also has an impact on resourcing and the sharing of ideas and strategies and ensures that no one year group is working in isolation, but is rather an invaluable cog in the wheel of the bigger picture.

So now you have your long-term aims tied up and completed through your vision statement and the curriculum map, the next step is the shorter-term plans.

Medium-term plans should not last half a term – this is incredibly tedious, tenuous and to be frank, boring for adults and children alike. Medium-term plans should be no longer than a couple of weeks so they are exciting and invigorating for all. Please don't go down the route of planning like this, saying: 'Oh, it's autumn so it's "All About Me" or "People who Help Us"', or 'It's spring so it's time for "Growing"'. There is nothing inherently wrong with these types of themes, but they do take over and have been done to death and you could easily fall into the trap of working to a plan rather than to the responses or interests of the children.

This more open and reflective style of planning, based upon assessment of observation, reverts back to the old mind map – building upon what the children have learnt and what they are interested in then linking in the learning opportunities. This is not an activity planner and in fact all planning should focus primarily on the learning rather than the activity. Winterbourne Infant School in Croydon utilises, very successfully, this shorter-term model. They use observations and dialogue to gauge what the children are currently fascinated in and then use this as a starting point for an exciting adventure. Planning at these schools is short term and reflective, a maximum of two weeks in advance based upon possible learning opportunities gleaned from observations and assessments. These plans are a continual work in progress, reflected upon daily and thus are organic in nature. Planning here often starts with interests and fascinations and fully involves the children in the process, it is in essence a true collaborative model.

The photo over from Winterbourne is a classic example of this collaborative short-term planning – the interest here was 'Pretending and playing in role through stories'. The three questions posed are:

1   What do we know about this?

2   What do we want to find out?

3   Reflective question on completion: What do we now know?

Photo 11. Collaborative planning display: Winterbourne Infant School, Croydon

Children's suggestions are placed on the display as starting points for learning, thus children's voices permeate the learning and they will be able to talk with confidence about their learning. It is possible to have two or three of these 'themes' running at any one time, but I would advise starting with one and gaining in confidence with the ideal before developing further.

This brings me back to a point I raised briefly about the model of enquiry. I noted that their planning always starts with an 'enquiry question' – the open-endedness of the learning opportunities are enshrined in a key question based upon either a fascination from the children, or something that the adult might bring to the classroom in order to inspire and excite the children. The open-ended question might be: 'What do we want to find out about?', or something more specific such as, 'Which is bigger, a whale or a diplodocus?' which could lead into a host of finding out and experimental learning opportunities.

Hale School in Farnham has introduced a wonderful system in the Reception and nursery classes which not only utilises the learning detective and learning hero models, but they also have a weekly review to capture the learning for all and leave threads for next week's excitement. This is visually displayed so parents have a clear idea of what and how their little ones are learning, thus engendering a greater sense of a learning community – just excellent practice.

Photo 12. Our week in Reception: Hale School, Farnham

Short-term or weekly planning

The final tier of planning is the short term, or the weekly plan. The best practice I have witnessed is where there are just two plans involved here.:

1 Adult-directed teaching – over the course of a week what am I going to teach the children? This will include focus inputs, and phonics

2 Provision and enhancement planning – following my observations and dialogues with all parties, how can I enhance the provision?

The latter planning is the most reflective and should be carried out on a daily basis, following the learning detective inputs and the dialogue around what colleagues have observed during the day.

Formats should be simple. This first example is for the adult input detailing all the adult-directed and focus teaching across the week and showing progress in the teaching. Differentiation can be shown as can targeted groups for focus teaching (remember that this is intervention, based upon what certain children need in order to progress).

The second format looks at the ongoing consolidation opportunities in key areas within the learning environment – you will note that I have not put down specific areas of learning, as I find these very limiting and believe that practitioners need to look at their learning zones and then analyse what learning and opportunities to practise skills could take place in them. On this plan you could also add the learning detectives and discrete challenge.

Adult input plan	Mon	Tues	Wed	Thu	Fri	Notes
Phonics						
Speaking and listening						
Mental maths						
Story/reading						
Learning detective focus questioning						
Focus 1						
Focus 2						
Focus 3						
Evaluation						

Figure 12. Short-term plan: adult input

You will also note that there is not a separate outdoor plan as you should be viewing both the indoors and the outdoors as one learning environment.

Provision planning	Mon	Tues	Wed	Thu	Fri	Notes
Role play						
Construction						
Creative						
Book zone						
Writing space						
Evaluation						

Figure. 13. Short-term plan: provision planning

Summary

In this chapter, we have looked at observation, how it feeds into assessment and planning and how they are interlinked. We have seen how your observational system drives your planning and structures to inculcate and develop learning behaviours and reflective practice. Believe it or not – planning should be fun! We have also looked at the development of the Learning Detectives and how these assist in developing confident and capable learners. In terms of planning, the most important aspect is to diagnose what the children need in order to bridge gaps and make progress, whilst at the same time developing language for learning and well-being.

5 Discrete challenges and shared success criteria

'Challenge' – children love challenge; they are naturally programmed to challenge themselves, or otherwise they would never learn to walk or talk – two of the most challenging skills learnt in their lifetime. Your learning environment should afford children a range of challenges, both physical and cognitive. Children learn by practising and embedding their skills in meaningful contexts. Skilful practitioners get this balance between child-initiated and adult-initiated challenge just right so the learning is seamless.

In this chapter, I shall be looking at discrete challenge, establishing success criteria and sharing this with the children and, in the process, enabling children to self-assess and building up the confidence to talk about their learning in detail.

Routines and expectations in a Reception class develop gradually over time. The end game is to ensure that all your children not only have a fantastic experience, but are confident, resilient and ready to carry on with their learning. As noted in the previous chapter, there is currently a focus on developing behaviour for learning within schools. The emphasis is very much on independent learning: children knowing what they are doing and why and how they can improve. You will need to put this into an Early Years perspective, the children are after all only four and five, but this does not stop you putting the structures and mechanisms in place so that by the end of Reception, children are confident to talk about their learning, what they have learnt, the skills and attributes they have used and how they can do the job in hand even better.

The previous section looked at learning detectives, the learning heroes and the behaviour for learning concepts – these are excellent ways to reflect on the learning and children, being children, will be only too happy to show visitors all their work and how they did it. Challenge, the focus of this section, builds upon these foundations and pulls the learning together.

Discrete challenge

There are some practitioners who may feel that discrete challenge, where ongoing challenges and opportunities should be *discrete* throughout the learning environment, is not in keeping with the EYFS framework. I would argue that discrete challenge is not only in keeping, but it also accentuates the characteristics of effective use of teaching and learning – notably thinking creatively and critically. The introduction of these more discrete challenges are part of your ongoing transitional plan: as children become more confident and capable, your responsibility is to challenge them further and getting this balance between child- and adult-initiated challenge is part of the process. The driving forces are independent thinking, responsibility and problem-solving: asking children how can we make it better and to predict and come up with strategies to overcome issues. Children cannot do this in isolation. The adult role is to facilitate these thinking and reflective skills through meaningful challenge within an enabling environment.

There needs to be a balance between child-initiated and adult-led learning (see Chapter 3, page 47). The role of the practitioner is to introduce children to new skills and concepts and take them on journeys that they might not have any experience of – to introduce them to the possibilities in front of them. Too often there is insufficient support for child-initiated learning and insufficient thinking on how to take the learning forward. Consequently, progress is limited as, by their nature, children do not know what they don't know. Giving them meaningful, fun challenges builds upon the learning, extends the thinking and lays the foundations for resilience, persistence and sense of responsibility.

How do these discrete challenges work? They are incrementally introduced throughout the course of the Reception year. They materialise as either extensions from adult input or child-initiated learning and form the basis of assessment, as you need to know what the children are capable of doing independently, but in the same breath you need to give them the tools with which to succeed. In essence, challenges are 'jobs to do' that the children have ownership of but know that over the course of a day or longer they need to have a particular go at.

There are times when you might misjudge the challenge, be it not challenging enough or over-complicated – I would urge you to reflect and concentrate on the processes of learning and the growing independence and resilience within the children. Ask the children how they feel about a challenge – was it too easy, too hard, what could we (children and adults) do to make the challenge even better?

If you look at the learning and teaching process as a triangle of inputs this will assist you greatly in moving children forward.

All three corners are interlinked. Here, we are focusing on the apex: the challenge.

How does this work? Through your ongoing observations and assessments you will have a sound picture of where your children are placed and what they need in order to move

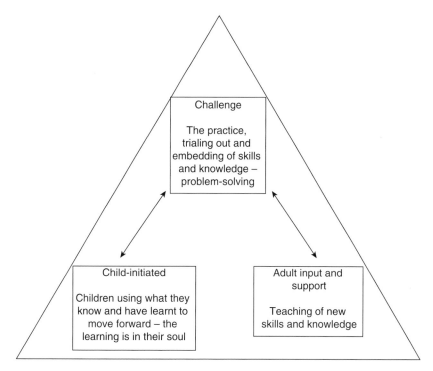

Figure 14. Learning and teaching process

forward. Some challenges may be child-specific; others open to the whole class where your differentiation is always through expectation.

In many of my schools this triangulated approach to learning and teaching is moving forward into Years One and Two. Hale School in Farnham, St. Peters C of E Primary School in Farnham and Park Mead Primary in Cranleigh have reported accelerated progress in the Infants, more confident children and greater accuracy of assessment by using this model. The reason is simple: children have the confidence and the understanding of what their responsibilities are, are proud to talk about their learning and any issues and are able to concentrate and persevere because this is how they learn.

I observed a wonderful example of a whole class challenge at Prior Heath Infant School in Camberley. It was in the run-up to Mother's Day. You know what usually happens here – a production line of children coming to the creative zone to put together a card for their mum based upon a template, with some poor member of staff stuck in the creative zone calling children over in turn. The result is a very bored adult, and thirty cards looking pretty much identical, with no individuality, interpretation or expression, and perhaps more importantly no differentiation or assessment possibilities.

In this instance, the teacher asked the children to think of all the things that mothers do and why they are so special to the children. There followed a quick use of talking partners and feedback to the teacher who scribed down some of the key words that the children had said on a flipchart and asked some children to come up and write their own words. So what we had from the children was an agreed statement: 'Mummy is special because... '

The teacher then very quickly handed out some sample cards to the children and asked the questions: 'Are these good cards? What needs to go in a card?' On another large sheet of paper, the teacher quickly scribed the children's responses:

- Needs to say who it is from
- Needs to have Mummy in it
- Can have a picture on the front
- Needs to say I love you in it
- Can be all colourful
- Needs to be able to fold in half.

Thus they had shared success criteria based upon the model of 'what makes good?' (which is discussed in more detail later in the chapter), stemming from the children themselves, and also an excellent shared writing opportunity. These two pieces of paper were taken over to an excellently-resourced creative zone where the children could self-select resources independently.

The challenge was set, using the 'must, should and could' model:

- You MUST make Mummy a card (this is non-negotiable, this is your responsibility)
- You SHOULD use some of these words in your card and other agreed criteria
- You COULD use some of your own words and try a different design.

Well, as you can imagine, the children did not just make one card, they made five or six, and with sensitive adult engagement and questioning chose the one they were most proud of. These conversations are of paramount importance because you will know your children inside out and should therefore know how you can challenge them further.

This differentiation through expectation is key to moving children forward. Differentiation should never be about outcomes; it is always process-based. Key open-ended questions to ask are:

- Are you pleased with what you have done – bring in your learning hero characters to further build up the reflection on how the children have carried out their learning and the attributes they have used (see Chapter 4, page 63)
- I like the way you have...
- Do you think...?
- What would happen if...?

These cards were then displayed on the working wall (this will be covered in more detail later), complete with children's voices expressing why they chose them and then taken home. This particular challenge was open for two days so children could revisit and refine their cards.

Excellent cross-curricular links were in place, opportunities for problem-solving within an enabling environment, ownership of the task and self-reflection. Some might say that the vocabulary of 'must, should and could'; is not particularly child-centred. I would argue that the words themselves do not matter, it is the principle that it important. The central purpose of the challenge is to coach a sense of responsibility within the children – that in life there are certain things that you just have to get on and do. The real learning is not necessarily the challenge itself but the autonomous decision and understanding that this is your responsibility within the context of the classroom.

Must, should and could

In some schools, 'must, should and could' has been replaced either by the 'chilli challenge' – starting with a mild korma, up to a hot jalfrezi – or 'hot, boiling and on fire'. I must admit I quite like this last interpretation and the sense of 'being on fire', mentally of course, when stretching and extending your own thinking and learning – bringing together a range of skills and knowledge in a fun meaningful context.

Being 'on fire' is equivalent to being in the 'zone' – the very small area where deep-level learning happens when skills and competency match the challenge. This comes about through detailed knowledge of what children are capable of, their skill and knowledge set and what they need to do in order to improve. Consequently the discrete challenges act as both teaching and assessment opportunities.

Iqra Primary School in Slough have fully embraced the challenge concepts, and over the course of a year more challenges will be in situ for the children to tackle. There is a great focus on writing within the challenges at the school. The photo below shows a rich writing area complete with the discrete challenge in the traffic lights on the left, the success criteria for writing a good sentence in the middle and supported by key words and prompts.

The challenge states:

- I MUST draw my favourite animal and write about it
- I SHOULD use wow adjectives
- I COULD write a sentence about my favourite animal

Here is an example of the end product.

Photo 13. Use of discrete challenge in a rich writing area: Iqra Primary School, Slough

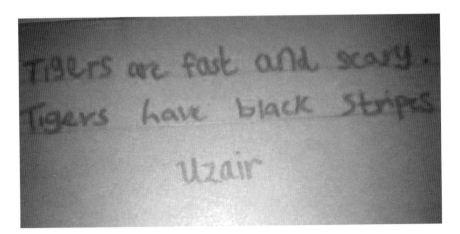

Photo 14. Descriptive writing example: Iqra Primary School, Slough

The child would then self-assesses their work alongside an adult against the processes of the challenge (the differentiation being through the teacher expectation) and also ask themselves key questions on well-being:

- Have I used adjectives in my writing?
- How proud am I of my endeavours?
- Have I challenged myself?

I think the answer to these questions is a resounding yes!

It maybe that throughout the course of the year more challenges are added so there might be three or four running across the week in the various learning zones, including outdoors. These challenges are then left out for the children to continue at their own leisure. The key point here is that children are learning roles and responsibilities at an early stage.

Challenge chests

At Lordswood School in Chatham they use the concept of 'challenge chests'. The challenge is within the chest: children open the chest to reveal the challenge and some of the resources they might need – not all of them as the expectation is that children find their own resources as you do not want to limit the possibilities within the challenge as the focus is on the process. Also in the chest are 'talking pegs' so the children can hear what the challenge is and the adult does not have to keep repeating themselves – again this is wonderful practice.

Shared success criteria

The concept 'what makes good?' is not a new concept. It allows children to reflect on their learning and is linked to positive assessment for learning. 'What makes good? can range from 'What makes a good listener' to 'What makes a good teacher?' – I personally like this challenge because it requires practitioners to reflect. In a number of the schools I support, the practitioners also ask the children what they expect from the adults. This question is often posed the other way round, where teachers consider their expectations of the children, and the children do not have a voice in the matter. Think back to the analogy I made in the introduction and Chapter 3, of likening the Reception class to your favourite shop (see Chapter 3, page 47). Are you offering your clientele (the children) the same deal?

Do not overdo the success criteria or challenges. Too often classes are littered with them. Less and in depth is definitely preferential. Likewise with the challenge, you do not have to have a piece of card on each and every table asking children if they can do something. This is overkill! Go for fewer high-quality challenges. This will allow children the time and the opportunity to go back and refine, to practise and embed new exciting skills and knowledge.

Celebrating success

Displays in Reception classes are key to celebrating successes for both the children and the adults. In previous chapters, displays regarding what the children are learning about, the weekly reflection and the learning detectives have been discussed. I ask you now to think of your own classrooms and the displays in them:

- do they act as learning and celebration prompts?
- are they active?
- do the children have ownership of them or are they adult-directed?

If in your classroom you have the three above displays in place, you are already surrounding the children with explicit learning. Children's voices are explicit and also any visitors to the Reception will be wowed because the focus is very much centred on the learning and enabling children to make decisions within the environment.

The working wall

The 'working wall' is a display that children have total ownership of. It is their display and they decide what goes on it. The photo below from The Grange Community Infant School in Addlestone is a wonderful example of a child-directed display.

So how does this work?

Each child has their own space on the display, and when they have done something that they are extremely proud of they may decide to put it up on the display, complete with explanation of why – bringing out the learning behaviours. So the focus is not on the product, because children will be at different levels of competencies, but very much on the processes of learning. Some children might not actually 'produce' much tangible evidence

Photo 15. Working wall: The Grange Community Infant School, Addlestone

Photo 16. Self-reflection and self-appraisal in action – challenge completed and success criteria met – let's get it up and on the wall!

Photo 17. The emergent working wall at Kingfisher Primary, Chatham. I'm particularly fond of the M People reference!

during the day and this is where your observations come to the fore, because you can utilise a photograph or an observation to act as a 'prompt for proudness'. For example, 'I saw today George that you were trying really hard to . . . .'

Children love this display because it is theirs! It does, however, need careful monitoring. For children being children will, if unchallenged, start to put up all sorts of 'old tosh'. Again differentiation through expectation is key, so when the children decide to put something on the wall – the key question to ask them is 'why? – have you challenged yourself – are you sure?'

Summary

In this short chapter I have covered the concepts of challenge and celebrating the successes of children. Discrete challenge, I would argue, is not an abandonment of Foundation Stage principles, it is rather an enhancement. Linked with your overarching vision for the outcomes of the children in your schools and classes, challenge adds an extra ingredient that fosters responsibility, independence, self-regulation and greater autonomy. The working walls, or whatever you wish to call them, act as invaluable evidence of children's progress across all aspects of learning – underpinned by a commitment to raise confidence and for the children to view themselves as independent and capable learners. It is a win-win situation!

6 Progress

'Progress' – agree with it or not, school is all about progress these days. Reception teachers need to demonstrate that all children make good progress and achieve well relative to their starting points. Personally, I do not see this as an issue, as all teachers want the best for their children and for the children to be the best that they can be.

It is worthwhile quickly making the distinction between 'achievement' and 'attainment'. The former looks at progress over time, the latter with the early learning goals at the end of Reception.

Schools will be judged on both of these. For the time being, attainment will be judged against the national scores and schools of similar make-ups. Achievement, until the implementation of the on entry baseline in September 2016 when a national picture will start to emerge, will be based upon rigorous teacher assessment.

The Ofsted *School Inspection Handbook* of July 2015 states that it will assess:

- 'the proportions of children who have made typical or better progress from their starting points, including disabled children, those with special educational needs and the most able

- the attainment of children at the end of Reception compared with Early Years Foundation Stage Profile national figures, including the proportion that achieve a good level of development, particularly in terms of how well children are prepared for Key Stage 1

- whether outcomes are consistent across areas of learning, particularly in the prime areas and the specific areas of literacy and mathematics

- how quickly disadvantaged children, and any groups that are underachieving, are catching up.'

Typical progress relates to a child, who, at the start of Reception displays the knowledge, skills and understanding that are typical for *their age* and consequently moves forward to attain a good level of development by the end of Reception. What you will also have to be aware of and report on is the percentage of children who, from their starting points, are on track to make typical or better progress. This more intrinsic analysis will support you in providing evidence that, despite lower attainment, all children and groups of children achieve well.

A child who attains a good level of development but who started at a lower level of development than is typical for their age will have made rapid progress. Conversely, a child starting school with above-age-related expectations who goes on to meet all the early learning goals but exceeds none of them is likely to be considered to have made insufficient progress. If you view 'typical' on entry to the Reception class as being at the top end of the 30–50 month band and the start of the 40–60 month band, this will give you a clear picture of where the children need to get to in order to show accelerated progress.

Age is the key component here. Children join the Reception classes at chronological ages ranging between your summer-born children at just 48 months and your autumn-born children at 60 months – a whole year difference, and thus they will be at varying developmental stages. Historically summer-born children, especially boys, attain less well at the end of the Foundation Stage – this is not surprising due to their chronological age and stage of development which can range from a whole year to 18 months behind other children. Whether or not it is sound or justifiable practice to judge differently-aged children against set outcomes and each other at this early stage is an argument in itself. At the end of Reception, the chronological age of children does not really come into the equation because the final figures concern the percentages of children who have attained the Early Learning Goals. It is, however, good practice to internally track the different-aged children to ensure that they all make progress and any gaps are rapidly narrowed – especially for the autumn-born children who might be chronologically 60+ months upon entry to the Reception but developmentally might be at the 30–50 secure level.

What constitutes typical progress?

There are many tracking systems available to schools, e.g. SIMS, Pupil Asset, Target Tracker, Classroom Monitor, to mention a few. Some schools have employed these, whilst others still utilise old-fashioned paper systems. None are right and none are wrong; it is what the practitioners do with the resultant information that is most pertinent.

Most schools now look at the developmental bands and break each of these down in three sections: whether a child is 'emerging' into the band, 'developing' within it, or 'secure' at it. These three descriptors can be viewed as 'jumps' of progress. Others add an extra + into the equation, so there is an 'emerging' and an 'emerging+', and so on; consequently there will be six jumps as typical progress across the year group. Again, neither is right or wrong, and schools who use the six-jump model argue it gives them extra insight and ownership of the developmental statements and allows them to fine-tune planning and provision.

Assessments are made through reference to the *Development Matters in the Early Years Foundation Stage* or *Early Years Outcomes* documentation (see Bibliography and Further

Reading) and through practitioner dialogue and expert knowledge on how a child is developing within a particular age band – whether the child is emerging into it, developing it, or secure at it.

To measure progress, practitioners need to measure the 'jumps' through the developmental bands children make. Taking the three jumps per band model.

- three 'jumps' of progress equates to **Typical Progress** in each year of EYFS – in reality this is Requires Improvement progress, as gaps will not be closed and the more able will not be extended.

- four or five 'jumps' of progress equates to **Rapid Progress** in each year of EYFS – as gaps are being closed and the more able extended.

The table below highlights the 'jumps' required in order for children to make rapid progress relative to their starting points –

For Child 1 joining Reception in the 30–50 band at 'emerging', three 'jumps' forward would only take them to 'emerging' into the 40–60 band – although this might be construed as typical progress, it is not enough as the gap continues to develop and the child is not working at an age-related level. However, four 'jumps' forward and the gap is being narrowed; with five, rapid progress would have been made. Consequently the school could report that although attainment might be low because the child has not reached the Early Learning Goal (for a particular area of learning) the achievement is good.

For Child 5, because they have joined the class in the 40–60 band at 'developing', anything below the exceeding statement would constitute insufficient progress.

The use of transition matrices such as the above, empower class teachers and leadership to set aspirational targets for the children and to highlight which children or groups of children require extra support and in which areas of the curriculum.

Do note, that those children whose base line is 'below', but not 'significantly below', are expected to catch up.

Age 30–50 months Development Matters age			Age 40–60 months Development Matters age			Early Learning Goals		
Emerging	Developing	Secure	Emerging	Developing	Secure	Emerging	Expected	Exceeding
Child 1								
	Child 2							
		Child 3						
			Child 4					
				Child 5				

Insufficient progress
Good/expected progress
Rapid progress

Figure 15. Table to show jumps required for children to make rapid progress relative to their starting points

It must be remembered that children develop in different ways and at different rates and often children's progress is in depth as they assimilate, practise and embed new skills and knowledge. So monitoring progress over time is crucial.

Once you have collated your data in your system, it is vital that this is analysed as your findings will allow you to plan for future provision, opportunity and intervention. I thoroughly recommend a half-termly summative action plan based upon your findings. I am indebted to Manorfield Primary and Nursery School in Horley for the summative plan shown in Appendix 2 (page 129). This example shows the summer term findings ready for transition into Year1, using the six jumps per band model – thus preparing colleagues for their new cohort. Best practice is to do this rigorously every half term and review the impact of any interventions and support retrospectively the next time you complete the process.

From the Manorfield Primary and Nursery School example (Appendix 2, page 129) you will glean a good picture of where your children are and where they need to get to – this is the next step.

As stated previously, it is not the system that you use that is important but rather what you do with the information it is giving you. Best practice entails this half-termly updates of progress to ensure that no children are left behind. Following your input of progress onto your system, reflection is required. A simple format will assist in this process and act as your medium-term plan.

For senior leaders it is best to produce an overview of progress through the year on the percentage of children at age-related expectation and the percentage of children on track to achieve a good level of development; the figures might not be the same but should show an increase over time – often electronic systems will produce this for you. Ensure you do this for all areas of learning so achievement is consistent across all areas and there are no glaring gaps in the data.

The Manorfield Primary and Nursery School analysis (Appendix 2, page 129) is an excellent example of reflective practice feeding into future plans, using the six-jump per band model of typical progress – you will note that on all the documentation there is a comparison from the Autumn 1 data set so the overall progress can be looked at throughout the year. Key groups are looked at in detail to ensure that gaps are closing,

On entry base line	Emerging	Good level of development	Exceeding	KS1
Sig. below	Typical	Accelerated	Accelerated	Accelerated
Below		Typical	Accelerated	Accelerated
Typical		Typical	Accelerated	Accelerated
Above			Typical	Accelerated

Figure 16. Transition matrix showing the aspirations from on entry and what is considered typical and accelerated progress

and as you will note there is an issue with progress across all areas for Pupil Premium children. The fundamental point is that all the team are involved in the analysis and future planning so that ownership is shared and the findings and implications are fully understood by all stakeholders. It is also important to ensure that governors are part and parcel of this process so they are knowledgeable about the processes and the intended outcomes.

Transition into Year 1 and life without levels

The transition matrix below is a useful tool for you to use to ensure expectations and aspirations are continued into Year 1. Here I have opted for a six jump per band model with age 40–60 months secure+ as equivalent to the ELG – as it can be safely assumed that if a child is secure+ at the 40–60 age band that they have attained the ELG. Taking six jumps (which is typical of children during this stage), you can see that Child 1 will have to reach Year 1 Within+ to show good or accelerated progress. Such a process will ease their transition into Year 1, and allow colleagues, with your summative plan alongside, to plan a developmentally-appropriate curriculum for children as they enter their new year group.

Again it must be remembered that children develop at differing rates and what we are looking at here is progress over time, and for some children to 'catch up' developmentally it might take a good two or three years. What schools need to show is that any gaps are being closed and the rigour they employ to catch and monitor this progress. It will be tricky for the next few years as schools get to grips with the new framework and expectations.

Year 1 on entry	40-60 months Development matters			Year 1					
	40–60 Developing+	40–60 Secure	40–60 Secure+	Year1 Beginning	Year 1 Beginning+	Year 1 Within	Year 1 Within+	Year 1 Secure	Year 1 Secure+
40–60 Developing+	Child 1								
40–60 Secure		Child 2							
40–60 Secure+			Child 3						

▢ Good progress
▢ Accelerated progress

Figure 17. Transition matrix to ensure expectations and aspirations continue into Year 1

You will note that I have not included the 'exceeding' judgement on this matrix as these statements are now outdated and incredibly difficult to measure progress through, as by definition 'exceeding' stretches on to infinity. The important thing to do is look ahead to the Year 1 curriculum for those children who have surpassed the Early Learning Goals

Old and new money: rough conversions of old levels and new outcomes through KS1

The table below is a guide linking old levels to the six jump per band model of progress through KS1 – it must be remembered that this is not an exact science and you will have to use your best fit judgement during the transition between the year groups. The table is extremely useful for Reception practitioners as it gives them the 'bigger' picture of where the children need to get to at the end of Year 2, and their important role in ensuring that the children in their classes have the best possible start to their school lives to ensure that the required percentages are working where they should be when they leave the year group.

Old NC level	Jumps
40–60 Secure	40–60 Secure
40–60 Secure+ (ELG or exceeding)	1Beginning
1c	1Beginning+
1b	1Within+
1a	1Secure+
2c	2Beginning+
2b	2Within+
2a	2Secure+
3c	3Beginning/3Beginning+
3b	4Beginning/4Beginning+
3a	4Secure/4Secure+

Figure 18. Old levels and new outcomes

Key questions for using your observations and subsequent data findings effectively

Gathering information	Summarising the information	Using the information
How do you ensure observations of day-to-day learning in a range of contexts?	How do you summarise a child's learning and development?	How do you organise the information so that it is understandable and easily accessible?
How do you involve all stakeholders – including the children and parents	How do you record your summaries?	How do you analyse the progress of specific groups of children?
What information is important and shows the 'unique child'?	How do you ensure that summaries are holistic and cover all areas of learning?	How do you analyse progress in all areas of learning?
How do you ensure your systems are manageable?	Who will you track and when?	What other information might you require and need to consider to understand needs and progress?
How do you support your team to reflect upon and act upon observations?	How do you quality-assure your summary assessments?	How do you identify and consequently act upon any gaps in provision and learning?
How is the understanding of children's needs and development utilised to support progress?	How do you identify next steps and show progress? How do you show progress so that it is understood by all stakeholders?	How do you collate any relevant information to support transition?

Development of language

The development of language should be at the core of Reception practice. It is a known fact that children are joining our Reception and Nursery classes at ever-lower levels of language development, both expressive and receptive. It is important to note that a language-rich learning environment, both at home and at school, has a greater impact on improved outcomes and progress for children than any socio-economic factors.

Schools must not be afraid of language and using complex words and sentences with Reception children. This is aspirational and sets the expectation in place for all adults working with the children. It is vital that all adults formulate the words and sentences correctly, using the correct grammar. You are never going to alleviate or negate regional dialects, and nor should you want to as these are part of a communities heritage and culture, but do ensure that adults speak clearly and articulately with the children, e.g. 'What was you doing?' is not acceptable. The result of this, if not corrected, will be that children will write as they speak and find accessing the curriculum increasingly difficult.

By the time a child leaves the Reception class they should have a working vocabulary of between 4,500 to 5,000 words and their subsequent meanings. This is an incredible amount of words. So, it is important that you demonstrate and model the language:

- for thinking
- for friendships
- for reflection and behaviour for learning
- for understanding and empathy
- for literacy
- for behaviour management, emotional regulation and well-being
- for the soul – language gives you access to wider possibilities, to communicate, to infer, deduct and comprehend.

DO NOT be afraid of language.

When your little ones leave your inspirational and aspirational classes at the end of the day you want them to be going home talking about the magnificence of their day, the challenges and the fact that their day was so outstanding that they have no superlatives to describe it!

Developmental milestones for language

These are the starting point and something that all your team need to be aware of and have in-depth knowledge of. The following table is a synopsis and originates from research myself and my colleague Heather Rick developed during our time spent working in Croydon supporting schools with transition issues and the development of language.

I would strongly recommend that you utilise the above tables in the construction of your curriculum development map mentioned in the previous chapter. This shows the aspirations you have for your children and the steps and reflective practices you are going to employ to ensure that they achieve your goals. A phonics tracker using the 'letters and sounds' is also extremely useful (see www.teachfind.com/national-strategies/letters-and-sounds-phonic-progress-tracking-sheet---2008–2009). I am grateful to St. Mary's Catholic Infant School, Croydon, who have kindly allowed me to include their *Progression of successful text reading through EYFS, KS1 and KS2* (Appendix 3, page 134) as an example for your reference.

How aspirational are you for your children?

I often have to ask practitioners in Reception, 'How aspirational are you for your children and do you set a ceiling on their achievement because of their situation?'. I cannot remember the amount of times I have heard teachers and practitioners say, 'Our children could not do that'. I always question WHY?

What are you going to do to ensure that your children have the possibility and the potential to do anything? Do not set a ceiling, whether wittingly or unwittingly, on what children can achieve because of their context – there is no excuse if you are aware of the children's needs and the strategies required to assist them become the best that they possibly can and are aspirational yourself.

I am privileged to work with some wonderfully proactive and forward-thinking schools and practitioners. In the next example I am indebted to Warren Mead Infant School in Banstead who have developed a fantastic system built upon high aspirations and expectations. In this school, the children are surrounded by shared reminders of what it is to be a good learner – focusing strongly on inculcating positive behaviours for learning and the key attributes the school are developing in their children and taking it back to their initial work on shared vision and values. Consequently, the children are confident to talk openly about their challenges and importantly the skills and attributes they utilised and were developing when they were working independently – the level and complexity of the language is truly outstanding!

Inspire, create, share

On top of this excellent practice, the school have also developed the 'inspire, create and share' concept whereby the children will firstly be inspired by something, it could be something that has come from the children themselves or something that the adult has introduced in order to extend the children's world. This is much akin to the 'enquiry question' model as alluded to earlier and utilised at Littleton Infant School in Shepperton. It is important that the inspiration is something multi-sensory in delivery, so the children can hear, feel, smell, see and taste it, thus linking in with the limbic brain. From this inspiration, the children then create something. This is open-ended as the resources and tools are freely available throughout the learning environment – this is open-ended learning in action, focusing on skills as the children refine and develop their ideas supported by an enriching and enabling environment and supportive adults. From this the children then share their ideas of products, focusing on the 'how' they did it, what was tricky and using other children's ideas on maybe how to improve it.

EXPRESSIVE LANGUAGE

Typical 2–3-year-old	Typical 3–4-year-old	Typical 4–5-year-old
• Two-word sentences, graduating to three-, four- and five-word sentences.	• By 3-years-old, children should have a confident repertoire of at least 500 words.	• 4-year-old children should have a vocabulary consisting of 4,500 words.
• Begin to use pronouns like 'I' and 'me' but not necessarily correctly.	• Uses sentences up to six words long.	• Communicates elaborate stories by putting eight or more words together.
• Emerging use of 'we', 'they' and 'it'.	• Uses words related to time and number, e.g. **three** fingers, **yesterday, tomorrow.**	• Narratives will now include imaginative and fantasy, not just the here and now.
• Pronunciation is clearer but strangers might have difficulty in understanding what is said and meant.	• Describes events that have already happened – uses an awareness of past tense, but will make mistakes with grammar e.g. 'wented' (went).	• Speech will be clear, but certain sounds may still be maturing: f/v/s/z.
• Starts to ask questions – usually starting with 'Where?'.	• Continues to ask questions moving from 'where' to 'why?'.	• Sh/th/l/r may well take into the fifth year to get right.
• Points to and names simple pictures.	• Enjoys simple slapstick jokes.	• Uses 'How?' and 'Where?' question words.
• Uses words to alert adults of needs and wants.	• Has difficulty with some sounds – r/w/l/f/th/s/sh/ch/dz.	• Can take turns in conversations and can resist the urge to butt in.
• Rapid growth in spoken vocabulary, from at least 50 rising to over 200 words.	• Can describe main story settings, events and characters.	• Generally uses sentences that are well formed but contain grammatical errors.
• Uses at least ten words consistently.	• Uses rhythm, intonation and phrasing to make meaning clear.	• Uses most sounds effectively – may have difficulty with some multi-syllabic words, or words with lots of consonant sounds close together.
• Talks aloud when playing with self and in a group.	• Can respond to simple instructions containing two items of information, e.g. 'Put the books in the tray.'	• Can continuing a rhyming string.
• Repeats familiar songs, rhymes and stories.	• Uses words to: give reasons, say what they want, play with others, direct others.	• Hears and says sounds in words in the order in which they occur.
• Carries out actions of rhymes.		• Uses talk to organise, sequence and clarify thinking, ideas, feelings and events.
• Fills in missing words to familiar songs and rhymes.		• Speaks clearly and audibly with confidence and confidence and awareness of the listener.
• Comments on things that have just happened.		

RECEPTIVE LANGUAGE		
Typical 2–3-year-old	Typical 3–4-year-old	Typical 4–5-year-old
• Will learn the meanings of an estimated one–two words per day. • Understands and can follow simple instructions, e.g. 'Give me the ball'. • Shows understanding and anticipates key phrases, e.g. 'I'm coming to get you'. • Attends to speech directed at them and listens to general talk. • Understands approximately 50 words and then supplements this with 5–10 a week. • Can pick out one or two objects from a group, e.g. 'Pass me the cup and the spoon'. • Follows directions, if they are part of a game or relate to immediate action, e.g. 'Feed teddy', 'Come and sit down'. • Can understand more words than they can use.	• Can listen to longer stories. • Understands words related to colour, simple number and simple time concepts. • Enjoys participating in 'make believe'. • Begins to understand and enjoy simple slapstick jokes. • Can take turns in conversations. • Understands who/what/where in simple questions. • Understands more complex statements, e.g. 'Put your toys away and we'll listen to a story'. • Can identify action words by pointing to the correct picture. • Understands simple prepositions and carries out actions. • Understands and answers simple questions, e.g. 'Where's mummy?'. • Can discriminate different sounds in the environment. • Responds to familiar sounds. • Understands more words than they can use. • Shows a sustained interest in picture books and can anticipate the next picture.	• Able to understand spoken instructions related to an activity without stopping what they are doing. • Can choose their own friends through personal choice. • Understands more complex language concepts, e.g. first/last/might/may/above/between. • Able to understand and carry out simple instructions with no obvious context, e.g. 'Go to the office and pick up some sticky tape'. • Begins to understand discussion about items that might have alternative uses. • Able to understand abstract questions, e.g. 'What would you do if?' • Listen to more complex stories with increasing attention and recall. • Listens to others in a small group and can participate in discussions. • Understands the use of objects. • Can identify an object with three or more critical elements. • Understands prepositions such as underneath/on top/behind/next to • Uses pronouns correctly, e.g. they/she/him/her/he.

Figure 20. Developmental milestones for language

The strength of this process is that it has inspired children to write and scribe their ideas and plans – as modelled by the adults. Resultantly, progress is phenomenal, both in an 'academic' sense and perhaps more importantly in a sense of 'can do' and pride. This has strong links with the growth mindset paradigm mentioned earlier in the book (page 41): children seeing themselves as confident learners and sensitive adults differentiating through expectation.

> 'The view you adopt for yourself profoundly affects the way you live your life.'
> (Carol Dweck, www.mindsetonline.com)

The following photos show progress in a half term in utilising phonics and writing – supported by positive 'marking' from the teacher.

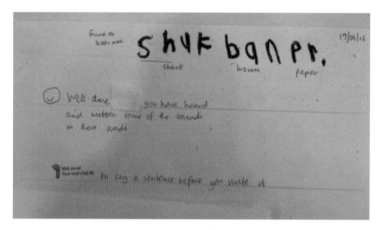

Photo 18 Plan to make a shark

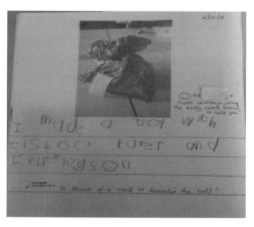

Photo 19 Six weeks later…

Getting it Right in Reception

This piece of work is a plan to make a shark (the inspiration) utilising brown paper – the writing shows the child has a grasp of initial and end sounds. Prompts from the teacher is reminding the child to say out the sentence before writing it.

This shows accelerated progress in both the physical manipulation of the writing implements but also the use of phonics in writing and the use of key words. Again, this shows positive adult feedback in extending the writing through the use of adjectives.

How does this happen? The answer is simple: through high aspiration, meaningful challenge, supportive adults and a rich and enabling environment.

Summary

Through this chapter we have looked at progress – what constitutes good progress, whether you are utilising a three or six jump per band model. We have discussed the expectations of progress and how to continue the tracking process into KS1. It is important to track children through all areas of learning as defined by the Early Years Statutory Framework as all have equal weight, but I would suggest that initially the focus in on the prime areas of learning and literacy.

We have also covered summative reporting and analysis on a half-termly basis to inform future planning and provision. It is important that you align your progress so that there are no gaps.

7 Leading an effective Reception class team

'Teamwork' – this is the crucial element in the Foundation Stage that can make the difference between children making rapid or accelerated learning and children making typical or inadequate progress. Perhaps nowhere else in the school is teamwork and shared understanding of values and principles as important as in the Foundation Stage. In essence, adults should be displaying and modelling the Characteristics of Effective Teaching and Learning in abundance. Are your team highly motivated, eager to have a go and show high levels of curiosity and imagination? Is there a relentless drive to improve?

There are two key questions to address here:

- How do you recruit an effective team?
- How do you develop and maintain one?

This chapter builds upon what was discussed in Chapter 2 when the concept of leadership in the Foundation Stage was introduced. In this chapter, we delve slightly deeper into the leadership role.

Recruiting and getting the best out of your team is a challenge to any leader. Ensuring you have in position the best possible people to take your vision forward is crucial to improving the provision for the children, the levels of involvement and well-being, and the quality of your team. Through my years of supporting schools and leading teams, I have found that the most important element is empowerment – getting the right people for the right jobs working at their highest level of competency. The juncture where challenge meets competency is where people will be working at their optimum level, be more in control and more likely to be a problem-solver and take ownership. A good leader will identify strengths within the team and put in place personalised support packages that not only develop the individual but also strengthen the core structure of the team.

Too often we focus on the negative aspects, instead of strengthening what people are good at or have a natural inclination for; we try and put square pegs in round holes.

How to recruit the right people for your team

Start by being very clear and concise in your definition of the role or roles and the responsibilities they will involve. What skills and attributes do you require for each identified role? If you start by looking at the skills required, rather than qualifications alone, you are more likely to recruit the correct person.

When working with young children there is a high degree of empathy and understanding required, alongside a developed sense of emotional intelligence. Your school's vision statement should be the driving force in the recruitment of any new staff, because the people that you are looking to recruit and develop must share the same outlook and philosophy as you – albeit at different levels – otherwise you will encounter problems and conflict because what you envisage in principle is not being carried out in practice.

Often you inherit an established team, with set principles and methods of practice. Some of these principles might be excellent and in tune with your own approach, but sometimes they might be at odds and reliant on routines and expectations that were set in stone in years gone by. You will have to take some time to sift through the practice, observing and monitoring the impact of provision and ascertain what can be changed immediately in the short term, and what might require a more long-term strategy of change.

Do remember that there's more to your members of staff than qualifications and skills set. Obviously a certain standard of qualification is essential, but do look beyond the obvious. Ask yourself:

- With the right mentoring, what could this person develop into?
- Is there the framework in place to ensure successful coaching and succession planning?
- Will this person gel with the rest of the team and your learning community?

I do believe that real life experience is vital. Too often schools are somewhat isolated from the outside world and can exist in a vacuum. As I mentioned earlier, it is easy to become institutionalised and simply do things because this is the way that they have always been done. I must admit that when I first left the relatively safe routines of the school and went back into independent work I initially found myself looking over my shoulder when having a cup of coffee and cheeky croissant in a coffee shop at 10.30am – would anybody see me!?

When recruiting staff, do take the time to allow them to explain their life experiences, for example how they might have surmounted issues and problems, what strategies did they use, how they formulated certain decisions and the impact they had on themselves as an individual. When I was recruiting members for my teams I was always looking for that 'something extra', an almost intangible element of character and fortitude – what value could this person add to my team; what skills and knowledge do they bring that might be different but at the same time are tuned in to a collaborative way of working?

Good leaders assimilate knowledge from others into their own vision – you cannot possibly know everything there is to be known about Reception practice and interpersonal relationships, so take everything you can from others to build up your own competencies – and remember that sometimes the greatest teachers do not always make the greatest leaders.

What will you need to successfully grow, develop and lead your team?

What you will need to inculcate and develop your team is a 'bias for action' – with active decision-making on behalf of all team members being valued, valid and appreciated, thus engendering self-confidence and independence of thought.

In a nutshell I term this 'initiative-based strategy' – a proactive not reactive state of leadership; one which fosters autonomy and entrepreneurship, developing innovation and nurturing champions! It is hands on, and value-driven with leadership showing commitment to all.

Often within structures, we place people in uncomfortable situations where they cannot operate to their full potential – I suggest that we 'stick to the knitting' and stay with the business that people know. The formation of this revolves around a simple structure: teams of people who are autonomous yet driven by centralised, agreed values. Any structure, it must be remembered, merely acts as a guide for where people should be to best fit any situation. Structures are, by their nature, very flexible and should be adapted as needed. Everyone should be familiar with the basic team structures, and leaders in particular must have an understanding of what the strengths of each member are.

The diagram overleaf, in simplistic form, shows how this works – matching up the competency of a person with the challenge/task you know they are capable of. Get this right and you will have involved and engaged team members. If, however, the task is too demanding and the competency not equal, you will get anxiety; conversely if the challenge is too rudimentary and undemanding and competency is high you will get boredom – neither of which are good. This system needs to be continually reviewed as competency and confidence grows. The role of the leader here is to scaffold and support, but also allow for freedom and autonomy of action.

This diagram, in simplified form, originates from the work of Mihaly Csikszentmihalyi and Maria Wong and stresses the importance of matching challenge and competency to ensure an individual can operate at their highest potential. I have used this theory working in the classroom with the youngest of children, working with senior leadership teams and even when coaching my rugby teams. The concept is simple – get the balance between challenge and competency right, because you have spent time analysing the strengths within your team, and you will have engaged and happy people because they will be

Leading an effective Reception class team

107

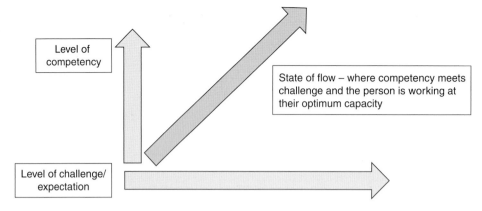

Figure 21. Competency versus challenge/expectation

working at the edge of their capacities knowing what they are good at and where they need to go next.

It is your role to try and engender this feeling of competency within your staff team and within your children. You will have no doubt experienced this feeling in your different roles – when time flies, things make sense, you basically crack on knowing that you are doing a great job – it is at this time when you are operating at your maximum level. I have to add a caveat here: this state of being is extremely tiring as it uses a tremendous amount of emotional and mental energy – so you, your team and the children, will have peaks and troughs of real involvement through the course of the day.

Usually this state is achieved through careful planning, discussion and intrinsic motivation. This is the most powerful form of motivation, when there is a desire to do the job at hand because it makes you feel good about yourself and the positive impact you are having on others.

I always refer back to the above model when undertaking appraisals, feedback and target setting for individuals in my teams – as you have to ensure the targets you set together are manageable, achievable and challenging and takes the individuals competency and skill level forward.

There are certain emotional responses and states that you, as a leader, will have to be aware of when working with and developing your team's competencies and professionalism; these might include anxiety, boredom, low morale, complacency etc. It is important to remember that members of your team, and by that I do include the children (for they are an integral part of the Reception team) will be, at different times, feeling all or some of the above. It is the leader's responsibility to pick up on the emotional moods of the classroom and ensure that there is a consistency of approach that allows all stakeholders to reach their full potential in a caring and supportive environment.

What makes a good Reception year leader?

If we return to the table introduced in Chapter 2 where we looked at Iram Siraj and Elaine Hallet's four themes of leadership and subsequent practices: directional leadership, collaborative leadership, empowering leadership and pedagogical leadership, we looked then in detail at the directional leadership in terms of developing the shared vision. We will now move on to develop some of the other themes.

The view of leadership is changing. The old hierarchical model of rank and subservience (which is still in place in certain areas and limits the capacity of individuals to fulfil their potential) is making way for a more democratic or collaborative model. This is especially so in the Foundation Stage which is primarily concerned with relational leadership with all stakeholders working together in a collaborative way to meet goals and improve practice, rather than being the sole work of one individual.

There are a set of characteristics of exceptional leadership. As a leader you will need to:

- **Be able to listen** – not just to the words people say, but to the meanings and inferences behind them. Good leaders spend more time listening than talking.

- **Be able to inspire** – through your everyday demeanor and how you dress professionally (but practically as you are working in a Reception class). How you use research to take the learning and teaching forward and are willing to try out new initiatives. Have high expectations of yourself.

- **Be able to nurture others –** being sensitive to others. This would be empathy in action – building up on strengths through a rigorous system of appraisal, but at the same time having exceedingly high expectations of others.

- **Be resilient and persistent –** keeping the faith. Do not allow external factors or short-term setbacks to divert you from your vision and mission. View setbacks as positive challenge and an opportunity for adaptation and review.

- **Be a clear communicator –**be clear and concise, using agreed language and not being vague in instruction and expectation so there is no opportunity for misinterpretation. You will need to communicate in different ways at times to individual members of your team – but what must not be lost is the consistency.

- **Be consistent in your behaviour –** this can be tricky! Every day is a challenge and you will have to develop a real sense of self so you respond to each challenge in a consistent manner. Teams respond well to consistency – they know what to expect and know that you are approachable. How you behave everyday will have ramifications on the behaviour of others.

- **Have a clear understanding of your strengths and limitations –** you cannot be great at everything; you must understand this and accept it. For example, I know that I am not a completer/finisher – I do get 'bored' when a project or focus is coming to an end – so I know that I will have to get someone in to finish the job off. Great leaders accept this and put in place around them people with different strengths to build up a cohesive whole.

Leaders in the Foundation Stage invariably possess a set of personal qualities, based upon secure pedagogical knowledge, emotional well-being and self-belief (which is not the same as arrogance), and skills, which, when combined, have the ability to influence and motivate others towards a shared and common goal. Leadership here concerns the creation of a set of conditions in which all stakeholders can give their very best within a supportive climate of continued reflection and on-going challenge.

In my opinion, good communication is key to leading a team in the Reception class. It involves listening, questioning, understanding and responding to what is being communicated within the classroom. There is a need to communicate on many levels, both on a one-to-one level and within the larger team. Remember that communication is not solely concerned with the spoken word – body language, posture, facial expression are all key, as is the manner in which you listen and empathise with others.

The key communication skills you will require are:

- listening and empathy
- summarising and explaining
- consultation and negotiation.

The knowledge you need revolves around:

- how communication works
- how you communicate best – no one is great at everything!
- ethics and confidentiality
- respect for others.

Reception and Foundation Stage leaders are, like most of the school leadership, in an unenviable position. The continued flow of new and updated directives, documents and policies from the DfE and Ofsted can often lead to information overload, and to try and lead on each new directive would drive you to distraction and result in unnecessary duplication. It also often results in abandoning a policy or a series of processes that work well within your team – do not throw things out that are proven to be successful. I do find it disheartening when I visit schools and hear about all the wonderful things they used to do and the positive benefits of these forgotten strategies which have now been superseded by updates and supposed new initiatives. Good learning and teaching and effective leadership has not changed in centuries – it is not about adopting new things, it is about being confident in your own beliefs and assessing how new ideas feed into, develop and support what you hold to be true. Your leadership role would be to summarise the new documentation, put it in a context of what you already do, and reassure all stakeholders that there is no conflict of interest or agendas which may lead to confusion and, at worst apathy and worry.

The ability to listen effectively is also key to your role as a leader and the direction you wish to lead your team – hence the vision and values exercise in Chapter 2 (page 31) is such a valuable tool in allowing leaders to listen to the thoughts and philosophies of others. Effective listening is not just hearing words but inferring the meaning behind the words. This is known as 'active listening', and to be an active listener you will need to devote time and space to the speaker – be they an adult or a child.

Monitoring your impact as a leader

I think it pertinent here to introduce a set of measures through which leaders can monitor their impact on the entire learning environment and all stakeholders within it and the quality of the learning on offer. They will greatly assist in developing your team and ensuring everybody is on the same track.

The children in the learning environment

There is a renewed interest in the work of Ferre Laevers and his Leuven Scale of Involvement (see *Well-being and Involvement in Care Settings*, F. Laevers). Through the on entry documentation, the 'well-being and involvement' levels of children are now being utilised as the underpinning principles of the characteristics of effective teaching and learning.

'Involvement' is a means of knowing deep-level learning is taking place. Excellent practice revolves around highly-involved children; if children are meaningfully involved in learning they are in 'the flow' – their emotional, physical and cognitive needs are being met; they are being sufficiently challenged and extended through engaging learning opportunities and supportive adults.

Involvement is a measure of quality, and as a leader it is an extremely useful and powerful tool with which to monitor the quality of your classroom and the learning opportunities within it.

Any involved child is totally absorbed in the activity and releases an immense amount of energy and consequently experiences feelings of great personal satisfaction. The source of this satisfaction is the inbuilt desire – the intrinsic need – for the child to gain a better understanding of reality.

So how do you know if your children are fully involved in the learning opportunities in the classroom?

The Leuven 'Scale of Involvement' is often utilised by practitioners to gauge the levels of involvement and the quality of provision. The practitioners consider how 'involved' the children are by thinking about:

- the levels of concentration they are exhibiting and how much mental and physical energy are they expending
- the levels of creativity and complexity there are applying to their tasks
- how absorbed they are in their learning opportunities
- the levels of persistence and resilience they show in their learning
- how well they can explain their thinking and reasoning
- whether they are quick to respond to suggestion and the learning environment
- whether there is a high level of talk in evidence about the tasks
- whether there is genuine excitement in the environment with busy and industrious children.

When observing, not all the signals need to be observed, but the essential ones must be present. The key signals are: concentration, resilience, creativity, energy, and persistence – these should link to your vision statement.

The practitioners assign a level from 1–5 to indicate the level of involvement for each child, where a level 1 shows little involvement, whereas if a child shows sustained intense activity this reveals greatest involvement (level 5) and subsequently excellent provision that is meeting all the needs of the child.

Unfortunately the involvement levels are often misused. Looking back to Chapter 4 where I discussed observations (page 63), you will remember that a quality observation is something that surprises and delights you – what this means invariably is that a child has been or is displaying high levels of involvement. Consequently, the majority of your observations will be of highly involved children. There is little point in taking an observation of a child at Level 1 or 2 on the Leuven scale because it is not telling you much about the child, it is telling you far more about the quality of your provision. I admit that I use the involvement signals and levels as an initial indicator of the quality of provision during school visits. If I see highly involved children in the environment, I immediately think that something good must be happening in the environment. Conversely, if children are at the lower end of the involvement scale I start to have serious concerns on the quality of provision and teaching.

Good leaders use the involvement levels as a monitoring tool – observing a number of children for a fixed time over a number of days and analysing the findings to start to paint a comprehensive picture of the provision offered to the children from a child's perspective. A child's lack of involvement will tell you that you have got it wrong!

The adults in the learning environment

Running parallel to children's involvement in learning is the role of the adult. Without doubt there are certain styles of teacher and adult engagement that are far more conducive to ensuring that the children are provided the opportunities for meaningful learning.

Any teaching or coaching is totally reliant on the adults in your team having a set of personal qualities and these should be part and parcel of your recruitment processes. Please remember that the quality of adult intervention is a critical factor in the quality of learning that is experienced by the child. I have looked at this in detail through my work with schools and can conclude that the most outstanding practice I have observed, and been privileged to support, occurs when there is in place:

- open dialogue between the children and the adults
- a genuine passion for young children's learning
- a partnership between independent and adult-led challenge and learning opportunities
- challenges and highly stimulating learning opportunities that motivate, embed and extend learning.

In addition to the 'Child Involvement Scale' as a method for monitoring, the 'Adult Engagement Scale' (see *The Effective Early Learning* Project, C. Pascal and T. Bertram and *Involvement of Children and Teacher Style*, (eds) F. Laevers and L. Heylen) is a useful tool and should be part of your monitoring schedule as it will lead to open, frank and professional dialogue, on-going professional development and agreement as to the role of the adult within the classroom.

According to Christine Pascal and Tony Bertram, there are three personal qualities to consider in the adults who are working in your team with the children: 'sensitivity', 'stimulation' and 'autonomy':

- *'SENSITIVITY: This is the sensitivity of the adult to the feelings and emotional well-being of the child and includes elements of sincerity, empathy, responsiveness and affection.*
- *STIMULATION: This is the way in which the adult intervenes in a learning process and the content of such interventions.*
- *AUTONOMY: This is the degree of freedom which the adult gives the child to experiment, make judgements, choose activities and express ideas. It also includes how the adult handles conflict, rules and behavioural issues.'*

There is a sliding scale of engagement, again running from 1 to 5, with 1 being non-engaging and 5 being totally engaging – what you need to be looking for is high-end engagement.

Leadership and monitoring quality

As part of your leadership role in the Reception class, you might also be the Foundation Stage leader as well. You will need to, as noted, monitor the quality of provision and its impact on academic and emotional outcomes for the children. The child involvement and adult engagement evaluations discussed above are part of this process. But there is more. The Ofsted *School Inspection Handbook* states in the 'outstanding grade descriptors criteria' (for this **has** to be your minimum expectation):

- *'The pursuit of excellence by leaders and managers is shown by an uncompromising, highly successful drive to improve outcomes or maintain the highest levels of outcomes, for all children over a sustained period.*
- *Incisive evaluation of the impact of staff's practice leads to rigorous performance management and supervision. Highly focused professional development improves the quality of teaching.'*

Here are some key questions that I use when preparing schools for any inspection. You need to be aware of these and to ensure your monitoring covers them fully – these will be extremely useful during an inspection, and it is important that you have evidence for them:

1. Leadership

- Where is it clear that you are meeting the needs of individual children identified through your initial on entry baseline assessment and subsequent tracking?
- How does your planning system show that you meet children's individual needs that have been flagged up in your baseline and tracking assessments?
- Can you talk through your monitoring of the Reception year and EYFS?
- What has been your impact on the development of the Reception class and the EYFS and raising outcomes for children?
- How do you ensure there are raising aspirations – how are transition matrices utilised to show progress and aspiration?
- What are the strengths and areas of development in the Reception class and EYFS?
- How do you engage in partnerships with other departments/schools? How does this support your leadership role and contribute to raising standards?
- How does your role as middle leader contribute to achieving the whole school aims?
- What systems are in place to ensure that children participate in a range of learning opportunities rather than just their favourites?
- How is the difference in challenge and expectation between Nursery and Reception in shared areas monitored and put in place?

- What is the percentage of below age related on entry – what evidence do you have to back these judgements up?
- What are the percentages of children on track for Good Level of Development (GLD) and for making inadequate/typical/rapid progress?
- How do you narrow the gap to ensure all children achieve as best they can?

2. Baseline and tracking

- Who contributes to the on entry baseline assessment?
- How do you use your tracking to inform your planning?
- Are there opportunities for a discussion about tracking with key workers/TA's, and what does this mean for the direction of children's learning?
- Is the on entry baseline assessment/tracking moderated across the team?
- How do you know your assessment is accurate?
- What are you doing differently in your planning to meet the needs of identified groups?
- What have you changed to accelerate the children's progress?

3. Outside area

- What is the connection between inside and outside learning opportunities?

In the event of an inspection, part of your conversation will be on how aware you are of the impact you are having on raising outcomes and improving practice in the Reception year. I believe that there are key areas that you need to focus on during your rigorous monitoring schedule. Ideally you should be monitoring specific aspects of practice and provision every week as part of your leadership release time. The team needs to be aware of these key areas and they need to be aware of what you will be looking at during the schedule.

It is important to stick to the schedule once you have decided upon it, otherwise any observation or monitoring can become random and haphazard in approach leading to limited improvement or purposeful reflection.

Leadership entails rigorous monitoring of the quality of provision, the adult engagement, the child involvement and the outcomes and progress of children – all of which can become slightly overwhelming and result in a hit and miss approach to monitoring the quality of your environment. Remember the Ofsted outstanding grade descriptors quoted here – I would suggest that you keep these constantly in mind when developing your monitoring and reporting schedule.

Over time, and working with many successful schools, I have identified seven key areas that should be the mainstay of your monitoring and evaluation:

1   Learning experiences within the wider curriculum
2   Learning and teaching strategies

3 Planning, progress, assessment and record-keeping

4 The quality of relationships and interactions

5 Inclusion, and British values

6 Parental partnership and community links

7 Physical environment.

The table opposite outlines the key areas that you, as a leader of learning and teaching, will have to keep in the forefront of your thoughts when developing and improving the quality of provision you offer children and families in your classroom. It comes with question prompts to assist in keeping your thinking on track, as I know from my experience that we can get sidelined easily and often the purpose of the long-term monitoring gets lost in the day-to-day incidentals that you will often come across – the long-term strategic monitoring is crucial.

These seven areas are by no means definitive, and you may well think of your own areas that you focus on, but they act as a rigorous starting point for further development and if presented to any 'visitors' will show that, as leader, you have a firm understanding of your role and responsibility and your impact on the quality of practice and provision in the Reception class.

I would strongly suggest that you timetable all of these dimensions into your monitoring schedule (see example below) so that over the course of the year you are continually analysing progress towards your shared goals, and putting in place supportive actions to achieve them.

You will never finish the job in hand – nirvana will never be reached, because as you evaluate you will always find ways and strategies to keep improving.

Your monitoring schedule should inform your action planning. Appendix 4 (page 135) provides an example of a targeted action plan based upon rigorous analysis of findings and key actions from an inspection. It is important that all members of the team are involved in the monitoring process and that there is transparency when taking peer observations with dialogues centred on professional development. It is also key to have your governors involved in the monitoring schedule so they clearly understand the machinations of the Reception class as well as your purpose and vision as to what constitutes good learning and teaching

Obviously the bottom line for great leadership is to ensure that all children make good or better progress from their starting points – this will be the judgement. So, you will need to ensure that you and the team are fully conversant with expectations and how to use data effectively to ensure that you give the children the best possible opportunity to achieve as best they can.

Data can be construed as 'boring', but in reality it drives your practice – all your systems are focused to ensure that the data picture you present is positive and is a true reflection of the quality of your provision and practice in the classroom. I have provided several useful tables to assist you in your data analysis and subsequent actions.

Areas for monitoring	This area concerns	What you should have in place in your class	Key questions for monitoring
1. Learning experiences within the wider curriculum	• The range and balance of learning activities provided, and the learning opportunities presented for the children • How the curriculum is interpreted to embrace, support and accelerate children's learning and development	• A balanced range of learning activities covering all areas of learning and development • Programmes that cater for individual children's needs and respect cultural diversity • Systematic procedures for planning and evaluating the delivery and quality of the learning programme • Appropriately-qualified staff in the development and delivery of the learning programme	• What areas of learning does the curriculum contain? • What is the breadth and balance of the curriculum? • How is the curriculum planned and evaluated? • How is the curriculum differentiated to meet individual needs? • How are continuity and progression achieved? • How far are cultural diversity and British values reflected in the curriculum offered? • Are appropriately-qualified staff involved in the development and delivery of the curriculum?
2. Learning and teaching strategies	• How the learning experiences are planned and organised to encourage learning and discovery through a balance of adult input, challenge and independent opportunities • The quality of the interactions within the class and the extent to which independence and autonomy are fostered and encouraged	• Active, play-based and interactive learning encouraging imagination, creativity and the ability to make informed learning choices • Confident, independent children with positive self-esteem • Opportunities for children to self-manage and to express their needs • A sensitive, stimulating team of staff that engages in negotiations about expectations for learning and behaviour	• How are the children learning? • How much child-initiated talk and dialogue is there? • What differentiated challenge opportunities are there? • Who participates in the learning, and what is the quality of questioning? • How are creativity, imagination and challenge fostered in the children? • Are the teaching styles consistent for all staff? • How do staff support the development of confident, independent children with positive self-esteem? • What role do the adults take in supporting the learning?

3. Planning, progress, assessment and record-keeping	• Who is involved in the planning process and how far the planning builds upon previous assessment of children's learning • How the assessment of children is considered and the methods of recording their learning and experiences are noted. • The accessibility and sharing of information. • How children are making progress	• Systematic planning that caters for a wide range of experiences and includes all staff, children and, where possible, parents in the process • High-quality systems for observation-based assessment of children's learning • Comprehensive but manageable records about an individual' progress and learning • Parental and children's views in learning records • Rigorous analysis of progress of individuals and groups	• To what extent are staff sensitive, stimulating and empowering? • Do staff engage in negotiations about expectations for learning and behaviour? • Are the systems in place for planning, assessment and record keeping fit for purpose and who is involved in these processes? • How does observation and assessment feed into and support planning and provision? • Do all staff know what constitutes good progress? • What systems are used for observation-based assessment of children's learning and development? • How is progress measured and monitored?
4. The quality of relationships and interactions	• The quality of all interactions between children and adults within the setting by assessing levels of 'child involvement' and 'adult engagement'	• An ethos which is open and inclusive for both children and adults • Systematic assessment of 'child involvement' • Systematic assessment of levels of 'adult engagement' • The use of these assessments to improve the quality of the children's learning experiences and set appraisal targets to raise outcomes for children • A written statement on behaviour management and, where appropriate, have a staff member with responsibility for behaviour management issues	• Is the ethos of the classroom open, democratic and participatory? • What is the predominant style of interaction? • What are the levels of 'child involvement' and 'adult engagement' and how are these utilised to improve provision, practice and outcomes?

5. Inclusion, and British values	• How learning experiences reflect, acknowledge and celebrate diversity, and the extent to which the ethos is respectful and inclusive	• The active promotion of equality of opportunity, racial harmony and anti-discriminatory practice for all children and adults • Appropriate staffing, physical environment and practices to allow those with special needs to access its services • An open challenge to all forms of discrimination	• Is there a written policy for equalities and anti-discriminatory practice for all children and adults? • How are equality issues addressed for children and adults? • How are the needs of children with disabilities identified and met? • How far is practice for children with special needs consistent with current legislation and guidance?
6. Parental partnership and community links	• On collecting evidence on the nature of the partnership with parents and the ways in which they, and other members of the local community, are involved in the learning process • Links between the school and other early childhood settings which the child may have attended previously are important	• Evidence of the partnership with parents, carers and the local community to meet the needs of the children • Information for parents about the school and provide opportunities for participation • Provide regular information about children's developmental progress, and make their written records on children accessible to parents	• Is there a written policy to support parental partnership? • In what ways are parents involved in children's learning? • How are liaison, co-ordination and planning with other settings achieved? • Does the school offer family support? • How is information about the learning communicated to parents?
7. Physical environment	• The use of space and resources, both inside and out, and the availability, condition and appropriateness of the learning resources	• Provide adequate space in an appropriate location • Be welcoming to children and parents, and offer access to facilities that support a range of learning activities which promote development, reflect cultural diversity and are inclusive for children with special needs • Provide furniture, equipment and learning opportunities appropriate to their purpose • Offer sufficient and incremental challenge	• How far is the accommodation safe, secure and suitable for its purpose? • Is the classroom welcoming, accessible and stimulating? • Are challenges explicit and will they extend children's learning? • How is the outside area utilised? • What is the rationale for the room layout? • What facilities and resources are available and how far do these reflect cultural diversity? • How do these nurture children's autonomy and their exploratory drive?

Figure 22. Monitoring and evaluation

MONITORING SCHEDULE				
Autumn 1	Teacher focus	Leader focus	Governor focus	Report and action
Week 1	Physical environments in the classroom	Physical environments across the phase		
Week 2	Settling the children in and taking observations	Quality of observations		
Week 3	Learning experiences and curriculum	Learning experiences and curriculum across the phase		
Week 3	On entry baseline assessment completed	On entry assessments analysis		
Week 4		Learning and teaching		
Week 5		Parental links	On entry assessments	
Week 6		Inclusion		
Week 7	Progress review	Planning, progress and assessment		
Autumn 2				
Week 1		Relationships and interactions	Physical environment	
Week 2	Continue the cycle through Autumn 2 and throughout the rest of the year			

Figure 23. Monitoring schedule

Summary

Through this chapter we have discussed the role of the leader in the Reception class – how to appoint and recruit the correct personnel using your agreed vision and values as your yardstick and starting point. We have looked at the personal set of qualities that good and excellent leaders display and model each and every day when working with their teams and things that you might need to develop on a personal level.

This chapter has stressed the importance of getting the right people in the right positions so their competencies can be matched to your expectations – therefore allowing them to work at a level that best suits their current level of development. The key here is to be always looking for that next challenge for people and ensuring that the support mechanisms are in place to allow them to reach a comfortable level in their work – not all

What is the data for?				
Identify strengths and points for improvement	Inform school improvement planning	Compare the achievement and attainment of different groups	Ensuring provision is responsive to children's needs	Support teacher performance management
What analysis needs to be made?				
Are all children making progress over time?	YES/NO	• Do practitioners have sufficient knowledge and skills in supporting learning? • Does the physical environment support learning?	WHAT ACTION MIGHT FOLLOW?	• Plan for CPD in improvement plan and performance management • Raise qualifications of those staff leading practice • Develop indoor and outdoor provision with age-appropriate and challenging resources
Is attainment in line with national data?	YES/NO	• Do all staff have appropriate expectations and aspirations for all children? • Are then any factors that might be involved (high SEND, EAL boys/girls ratio)?		• Plan for CPD in improvement plan and performance management • Identify and implement strategies to meet children's needs
Are any particular groups falling behind and in which area?s	YES/NO	• Are there factors in common for children making less than typical progress? • Are there SEND children who have yet to be identified or effectively responded to?		• Identify and implement strategies to meet children's needs • Obtain support from professionals and ensure SEND procedures are robust and practitioners supported to meet the needs of children
Are there children who are making rapid progress beyond the ELGs?	YES/NO	• Are staff aware of the needs and abilities of all children? • Is there sufficient stimulation and challenge to support the more able?		• Review and develop observational assessment and responsive planning to ensure there is sufficient challenge
Are children making greater progress in some areas of learning than others?	YES/NO	• Do staff have sufficient knowledge and understanding and give equal attention to all areas of learning? • Does the learning environment offer rich and stimulating learning opportunities across all areas?		• Arrange CPD on identified areas for learning • Review routines and planning • Audit learning opportunities and resources in the learning environments.

Figure 24. Some suggestions for how to use data effectively and support for developing the team

Leading an effective Reception class team

will want to keep striving on, some will feel a sense of personal pride at different levels of responsibility and competency.

I have discussed the importance of monitoring the quality of provision and practice on a regular basis and prompts for leaders when analysing children's progress and the overall quality of provision.

Leaders need to be proactive and utilise a set of tools to ensure that they know exactly what is going on in their classrooms and that everybody is pulling together in the same direction – it is a difficult and demanding job as it separates leaders from former work colleagues, and this can be challenging for some as personal relationships do change because expectations and responsibilities alter.

The action plan in Appendix 4 (page 135) is an excellent example of reflective leadership in action, picking up on progress measures, monitoring of the quality of provision and putting in measurable steps to keep the momentum moving forward.

As a final point, I will raise the issue of succession planning – for when a team is performing to its utmost, some members might have reached their ceiling within the school and look for opportunities to develop elsewhere. This is just a fact of professional life and in reality is a positive reflection on you as a leader and developer of people, so do not be disheartened when people leave for new challenges – see it as a positive, that you are doing a great job. It is important that you are continually developing all members of the team.

Conclusion

I have thoroughly enjoyed writing this book, and I do hope that as Reception practitioners you have found it interesting and informative. My aim was to write it in a sequential manner, starting with an overview of Ofsted and the requirements within it and moving on to getting your vision and values in place as all else will grow from these, and they are your continual reference points, so when supposedly new initiatives and directives arrive you will have the confidence to place them within the context of your vision of what constitutes excellence in the Reception year.

The chapters follow in a rough developmental chronological order, establishing routines, environments and expectations. I have introduced discrete challenge and a number of extremely useful strategies to ensure you are building up children's behaviour for learning and self-confidence. I have concluded with a section on leadership and developing the role of leaders in the Reception so they are confident in their role and have full accountability of their provision.

I would urge you to focus on one chapter at a time in your own personal development and use this book as a guidance for strategies. I wouldn't recommend trying to cover all the chapters in one go as the elements of practice suggested will need to be practised, embedded and reviewed prior to moving on.

What I do know, is that the suggestions and strategies in this book have proved immensely successful in developing teacher's professionalism, raising outcomes for children and narrowing of achievement and attainment gaps in many schools across the country.

I do hope that you will find many of the suggestions useful, but the important thing is to gain ownership of them – what I have offered here are some strong and proven guidelines, a skeleton if you like, for you to flesh out in your own schools and with your own children.

Enjoy them, practise them and you will end up having a truly great Reception class!

Appendices

Appendix 1: Sample aspiration, skills and development map across the Foundation Stage

Aims:

- To ensure that all nursery children have secure pre-literacy skills by the time they leave nursery
- To ensure that the percentage of children in Reception who achieve a good level of development is above national average
- To ensure that there is clear evidence of differentiation, challenge, support and developmental marking in children's learning
- To ensure that there is a broad and rich diet of literacy and numeracy experiences for all children in the EYFS
- To ensure that all children make rapid progress relative to their starting points and the gap continues to be narrowed
- To ensure that there is a range of evidence in the EYFS portfolios to support judgements.
- Speaking and listening

Nursery aspirational outcomes	<ul><li>Develop as attentive, active listeners</li><li>Speak confidently, clearly and audibly to adults and children</li><li>Hear and continue a rhyming or alliterative string</li><li>Use language in creative role play and negotiation/interaction with others</li></ul>	
Autumn	**Spring**	**Summer**
<ul><li>Follow simple instructions</li><li>Talk and listen in a small group</li><li>Know three nursery rhymes by heart</li><li>Retell simple events in the correct order</li><li>Speak in complete 5/6 word sentences</li></ul>	<ul><li>Ask and answer questions</li><li>Begin to use 'and', 'because' and familiar story language</li><li>Start to speak and listen in a larger group</li><li>Know five nursery rhymes by heart</li><li>Use role play to re-enact roles</li><li>Listen and talk to response partner</li></ul>	<ul><li>Listen and talk in whole class sessions</li><li>Work with other(s) collaboratively</li><li>Use language, props and puppets in role play to create or recreate familiar roles</li><li>Know seven nursery rhymes by heart</li><li>Identify and continue rhyme/alliteration</li><li>Begin to hear the last sound in a word</li></ul>

Reception aspirational outcomes	• Listen actively • Confidently contribute ideas and suggestions; answer questions in group and class discussions • Speak confidently in a range of situations • Hear and identify phonemes in words (segment and blend)		
Autumn	**Spring**	**Summer**	
• Know six stories orally by heart • Identify, continue and create rhyming and alliterative string • Listen and respond in whole class • Talk and listen to response partner • Ask and answer questions in class • Speak aloud in front of an audience • Orally segment and blend cvc words • Phase 2 letters and sounds completed	• Know ten stories by heart • Express own ideas • Rehearse prior to writing • Use vocabulary such as 'then', 'and', 'because' to extend sentences • Begin to create own stories • Phase 3 letters and sounds completed	• Know 15 stories by heart • Give an explanation or set of instructions • Use wider, topic-specific vocabulary • Ask if unsure what new vocabulary means • Join a discussion and give an opinion • Phase 3 letters and sounds consolidated • Phase 4 letter and sounds completed	

Reading			
Nursery aspirational outcomes	• Enjoy being read to • Handle books carefully • Talk about favourite stories • Act out, use props/instruments to retell or create stories		
Autumn	**Spring**	**Summer**	
• Listen to stories • Join in repetitive phrases in small group • Select and look after books carefully • Turn the pages in books carefully • Hold book the right way up • Have had prediction modelled	• Name and discuss characters in books • Have a favourite story • Begin to predict what may happen next • Say what part of book was liked • Join in retelling using props or puppets	• Aspects 1–6 of letters and sounds have been covered • Talk about the characters and setting • Begin to offer opinions about a book • Use story language in role play • With pictures and support can retell story • Begin to recognise some familiar words	
Reception aspirational outcomes	• Read simple books independently using a range of cues – picture, context, phonic, graphic • Can build on story model, creating own story • Can read a range of genres • Talk about what they have read or listened to, recount with aid of pictures and discuss their feelings • Answer 'on the line' questions and begin to answer more probing questions		

Autumn	Spring	Summer
• Know six stories by heart • Use picture cues and context to 'read' a story • Answer on the line questions • Adults are modelling answering • Questions using four question stems • Join in with repeated refrains; predict words using rhyme • Oral blending of cvc words • Use story language in role play • 'Read' stories and lists	• Know 12 stories by heart • Blend and read cvc words • Read simple sentences • Begin to read fiction, poetry and non-fiction • Talk as a character • Retell stories independently using role play and props/puppets • Use stories as a basis for creating own with support • Phase 2 letters and sounds completed • Phase 3 letters and sounds begun	• Read simple books and know 15 by heart • Discuss the plot, setting, characters • Give opinions about books read or listened to • Decode unfamiliar words from Phase 3 and 4 letters and sounds • Read common irregular words • Predict how a story may end • Read a range of genres • Create own stories based on those known

Writing		
Nursery aspirational outcomes	• Develop fine motor control • Hold pencil correctly • Draw/paint reasonably accurate, detailed figures • Write name using school script	
Autumn	**Spring**	**Summer**
• Paint and draw, begin to be challenged to refine detail • Focus on gross motor skills • Work with play-dough to strengthen hands	• Fine motor exercises to strengthen fingers • Correct pencil grip • Dot–to–dot, pre-writing patterns • See writing being written and read	• Aspects 1–6 of letters and sounds have been covered • Differentiate between picture and print • Know print is read and conveys meaning • Write own name in cursive script • People have head, body, arms and legs, eyes, nose, mouth, ears and hair
Reception aspirational outcomes	• Use school script, joining blends, di- and tri-graphs • Write a golden sentence independently • Write a longer piece of text, with evidence of communication and language • Write a range of genres (story, list, label, caption, recount, instructions) • Segment words, including those with adjacent consonants or vowels	

Autumn	Spring	Summer
• Fine motor exercises (tweezers, 'playing piano' etc.) • Pre-writing patterns, dot-to-dot and colouring in • Write name in cursive script • Oral segmenting of cvc words • Drawings are more detailed and coloured in and are more neatly completed	• Sentence rehearsed orally prior to writing • Write golden sentence(s) • Sentence read back to check • Beginning to write in range of genres • Phase 3 letters and sounds completed • Can spell and write 'the', 'to', 'I', 'no', 'go' • Digraphs and blends joined	• Make phonetically plausible attempts at words from Phase 3 and 4 • Can spell and write 'he', 'she', 'we', 'me', 'be', 'was', 'my', 'you', 'her', 'they', 'all', 'are' • Write longer texts • Genres: story, list, label, caption, explanation and instructions • Beginning to read through work to check • Adds connectives and adjectives to writing

Numeracy	
Nursery aspirational outcomes	**Work within 10** • 1:1 correspondence and accurate counting established • Use practical resources to add, subtract, share and multiply, solve problems • Be able to explain their thinking and working • Vocabulary: how many, altogether, makes, add, more, take away, left, bigger, smaller, heavier, lighter, longer, shorter, taller, next, after, in, on, under, beside, round, straight

Autumn	Spring	Summer
• Join in counting rhymes and songs • Work within 3 practically to add, take away, count and problem solve • 1:1 correspondence, accurate counting • Use direct comparison to compare size • Vocabulary: how many, count, bigger, • smaller, in, on, round, straight • Match items that are the same	• Work within 5 practically to add, take away, count and problem solve • Directly compare length/height • Vocabulary: altogether, makes, add, take away, longer, shorter, taller, fair, unfair, under, next to, next • Sort items by given criterion • Continue a two-element pattern	• Work within 10 practically to add, take away, count and problem solve • Directly compare mass, shapes • Vocabulary: how many more/ left, heavier, lighter, after, before, beside • Begin to record mathematics practically • Begin to suggest own criterion for sorting

Reception aspirational outcomes	**Work within 20** • 1:1 correspondence and accurate counting established • Use practical items to add, subtract, share and multiply and problem solve, explain thinking • Use number line to add and subtract • Vocabulary: circle, square, rectangle, triangle, cube, cuboid, sphere, cone, total, leaves, before, fair, unfair, next to, curved, corner, side, edge, equal, the same as, opposite • Begin to record mathematics pictorially, practically and using written representation • To use direct comparison and non-standard units to measure and rank items • Sort items by given criterion, begin to suggest own criterion

Autumn	Spring	Summer
• Within 10, practical activities, problems • Begin using numerals 0–10 to match set • Adult model recording strategies • Create a two-element pattern • Name, match and describe common 2D shapes • Use direct comparison to measure	• Within 15 • Recording calculations, children solve given calculations, use practical resources, number lines to jump on • Name, match and describe common 3D shapes • Use non-standard units	• Within 20 • Read and solve written calculations, choosing resources • Record own calculations using +, -, = • Consolidate work on shape, measure and pattern

Appendix 2: End of year data analysis: Attainment – achievement of good level of development by courtesy of Manorfield Primary and Nursery School, Horley

		Autumn 1		Summer 2		Difference
		On track (to achieve expected)	Not on track (for expected)	On track (2 or 3)	Not on track to achieve expected (1)	
Prime areas of learning	Listening and attention	31%	69%	76%	24%	45%
	Understanding	31%	69%	72%	28%	41%
	Speaking	29%	71%	76%	24%	47%
	Moving and handling	34%	66%	93%	7%	59%
	Health and self-care	34%	66%	86%	14%	52%
	Self-confidence and self-awareness	49%	51%	83%	17%	44%
	Managing feelings	41%	59%	86%	14%	45%
	Making relationships	37%	63%	86%	14%	51%
Specific areas of learning	Literacy (reading)	21%	79%	72%	28%	51%
	Literacy (writing)	21%	79%	72%	28%	51%
	Number	24%	76%	72%	28%	38%
	Shape Space and Measure	28%	72%	76%	24%	48%

Data analysis for those children achieving 'expected or exceeding' (2 or 3) – Gender gap Autumn 1 to Summer 2
By courtesy of Manorfield Primary and Nursery School, Horley

		Autumn 1 (29)	Boys (16)	Girls (13)	Summer 2 (29)	Boys (16)	Girls (13)	Difference	
								Autumn	Summer
Prime areas of learning	Listening and attention	31%	25%	69%	76%	63% 10	92% 12	44%	29%
	Understanding	31%	25%	69%	72%	63% 10	92% 12	44%	29%
	Speaking	29%	25%	69%	76%	69% 11	85% 11	44%	16%
	Moving and handling	34%	44%	62%	93%	94% 15	92% 12	18%	2%
	Health and self-care	34%	44%	62%	86%	81% 13	92% 12	18%	11%
	Self-confidence and self-awareness	49%	44%	69%	83%	75% 12	92% 12	24%	17%
	Managing feelings	41%	44%	69%	86%	69% 11	85% 11	24%	16%
	Making relationships	37%	44%	69%	86%	81% 13	92% 12	24%	11%
Specific areas of learning	Literacy (reading)	21%	25%	62%	72%	63% 10	85% 11	37%	22%
	Literacy (writing)	21%	25%	62%	72%	63% 10	85% 11	37%	22%
	Number	24%	25%	62%	72%	63% 10	85% 11	37%	22%
	Shape Space and Measure	28%	25%	62%	76%	69% 11	85% 11	37%	16%

Data analysis for those children achieving 'expected or exceeding (2 or 3)' Pupil Premium/non Pupil Premium Autumn 1 to Summer 2
By courtesy of Manorfield Primary and Nursery School, Horley

		Autumn 1 (29)	PP (9)	Non-PP (20)	Difference Autumn	Summer 1 (29)	PP (9)	Non-PP (20)	Difference Spring
Prime areas of learning	Listening and attention	45%	33%	50%	17%	76%	55% 5	85% 17	30%
	Understanding	45%	33%	50%	17%	72%	44% 4	85% 17	41%

	Speaking	45%	44%	50%	6%	76%	44% 4	90% 18	46%
	Moving and Handling	52%	33%	60%	27%	93%	77% 7	100% 20	23%
	Health and self-care	52%	33%	60%	27%	86%	66% 6	95% 19	29%
	Self-confidence and self-awareness	55%	44%	60%	16%	83%	66% 6	90% 18	24%
	Managing feelings	55%	44%	60%	16%	86%	55% 5	100% 20	45%
	Making relationships	55%	44%	60%	16%	86%	66% 6	95% 19	29%
Specific areas of learning	Literacy (reading)	41%	22%	50%	28%	72%	33% 3	90% 18	57%
	Literacy (writing)	41%	22%	50%	28%	72%	33% 3	90% 18	57%
	Number	41%	22%	50%	28%	72%	33% 3	90% 18	57%
	Shape Space and Measure	41%	22%	50%	28%	76%	44% 4	90% 18	46%

Measuring progress across the Reception year
By courtesy of Manorfield Primary and Nursery School, Horley
Expected progress being six jumps per band

Area of learning		Six or more jumps of progress whole class (29)	Boys (16)	Girls (13)	Pupil Premium children (9)	Non-Pupil Premium children (20)
Prime areas of learning	Listening and attention	86%	88%	85%	56%	100%
	Understanding	86%	88%	85%	67%	95%
	Speaking	83%	81%	85%	67%	90%
	Moving and handling	79%	69%	92%	67%	85%
	Health and self-care	97%	94%	100%	89%	100%
	Self-confidence and self-awareness	79%	69%	92%	56%	90%
	Managing feelings	83%	75%	92%	67%	90%
	Making relationships	93%	94%	92%	78%	100%
Specific areas of learning	Literacy (reading)	90%	88%	92%	89%	90%

	Literacy (writing)	72%	75%	69%	67%	75%
	Number	72%	69%	77%	44%	85%
	Shape space and Measure	76%	69%	85%	44%	90%

Home-grown children (those who also attended our nursery)
By courtesy of Manorfield Primary and Nursery School, Horley

	Home-grown children	Non-home-grown children
% of children achieving 'Good Level of Development'	**71%**	**51%**
% of children making six+ steps of progress in the Reception year		
Listening and attention	90%	83%
Understanding	86%	81%
Speaking	83%	74%
Moving and handling	62%	59%
Health and self-care	83%	75%
Self-confidence	86%	77%
Managing feelings	86%	75%
Making relationships	90%	80%
Literacy (reading)	66%	54%
Literacy (writing)	66%	54%
Number	66%	58%
Shape Space and Measure	72%	68%

Summary of information gathered at end of year data analysis
By courtesy of Manorfield Primary and Nursery School, Horley

Summary of information gathered at end of year data analysis				
What is the data telling us	What we need to do	Who will be involved	How often	Impact
69% of children have achieved 'Good Level of Development' (GLD)	Celebrate success of higher GLD achievement than last year, set new, more aspirational target for next year's GLD.	Class teacher and identified support		

Children making rapid progress since Sept (seven+ steps in the three prime areas is good) **Communication and Language:** Listening and attention – 72% Understanding –72% Speaking – 62% **Physical Development:** Moving and handling– 59% Health and self-care – 93% **PSED:** Self-confidence and self-awareness – 62% Managing feelings and behaviour – 69% Making relationships – 72%	In transition meetings analyse data for new cohort; look at areas for improvement/ of concern – set targets and interventions for the class in Year 1 depending on needs.	Class teacher and identified support	Transition meeting before summer; pupil progress meetings half-termly thereafter	Children that were emerging the ELG's will have set interventions where they will make rapid progress and be working at age-related expectations by Christmas
Small number of children have made slow progress (five steps and lower) from Autumn 1 to Summer 2 in prime areas: **Communication and Language:** Listening and attention – 7% Understanding – 3% Speaking – 3% **Physical Development:** Moving and handling – 17% Health and self-care – 0% **PSED:** Self-confidence and self-awareness – 17% Managing feelings and behaviour – 14% Making relationships – 3%	Identify those children to be in intervention groups in Year 1	Class teacher and identified support	Transition meeting before summer; pupil progress meetings half-termly thereafter	Children making slow progress across the year will be identified earlier and smart interventions put into place to ensure they achieve at least typical progress from their starting points
All of the children failing to progress at the expected rate in prime areas are those who have EAL, IPMs or Pathway plans	Ensure SENDCo and Year 1 team are creating smart pathway plans/ IPMs to ensure these children make rapid progress in Year 1	Class teacher and identified support	Transition meeting before summer; pupil progress meetings half-termly thereafter	Children making slow progress across the year will be identified earlier and smart interventions put into place to ensure they achieve at least typical progress from their starting points
There is a considerable gap between boys and girls achieving GLD (boys – 56%, girls 85%) 55% of the boys who did not achieve GLD have SEN and have made good progress since their starting points 22% of the boys who didn't achieve GLD have EAL with specific interventions to support their needs, but were still not achieving the expected levels in speaking, therefore were not able to achieve in reading or writing and some Communication and Language aspects.	Ensure staff in Year 1 (and in early years for future cohorts) understand the boy's interests in their key groups and plan accordingly to them See action plan for other actions to tackle underachievement in boys	Whole of early years and Year 1 team	Key stage meetings planned for first half term to address boys achievement	The gap between the achievement of GLD in boys and girls will have closed by at least 15%

Appendix 3: Progression of successful text reading through EYFS, KS1 and KS2
Courtesy of St. Mary's Catholic Infant School, Croydon

Band/ colour	Reading recovery level	Approximate phonic phase	New NC level	YR	Y1	Y2	Y3	Y4	Y5	Y6
1 PINK	1, 2	Phase 2	40–60 Developing	▓						
2 RED	3, 4, 5	Phase 3	40–60 Secure	░	▓					
3 YELLOW	6, 7, 8	Phase 3/4	40–60 Secure+	░	░					
4 BLUE	9, 10, 11	Phase 4/5	1Secure	░	░					
5 GREEN	12, 13, 14	Phase 5	1Secure+/ 2Beginning		░	▓				
6 ORANGE	15, 16	Phase 5/6	2Beginning+		░	░				
7 TURQUOISE	17, 18	Phase 5/6	2Wworking within/ 2Working within+		▓	░	▓			
8 PURPLE	19, 20	Phase 6	2Secure/ 2Secure+			░	░			
9 GOLD	21, 22	Phase 6	3Beginning/ 3Beginning+				░	░		
10 WHITE	23, 24	N/A					░	░		
11 LIME		N/A						░	░	▓
Not banded at present		N/A						░	░	░
Not banded at present		N/A						▓	░	

KEY   Majority of children secure at this level ░

Normal range of achievement ▓

Appendix 4: Example action plan
Courtesy of Manorfield Primary and Nursery School, Horley

Priority 1: Improve the pupils' progress and outcomes

Success criteria:

76% of children will achieve 'Good Level of Development' (GLD) at the end of Reception

All teaching in the Foundation Stage will be graded at least 'Good'

Tracking shows that all children are making greater than typical progress from their starting points

Gaps between Pupil Premium and non-Pupil Premium will be significantly reduced with an aspirational minimum of 70% of Pupil Premium children achieving GLD at the end of Reception

70% of children will leave pre-school working at age-related expectations. Gaps in attainment will be significantly reduced with a greater percentage leaving the pre-school at age-related expectations

Objective	School/LA Actions	Milestones	Lead	Action target date	Outcome/S. Criteria	Monitoring
To ensure 'challenge' is planned for, implemented in learning opportunities and becomes an integral part of the teaching in Early Years to ensure rapid progress and 76% of children leave with GLD.	Reception to continue to develop learning detectives to link with the 'challenges' set around the unit for ensuring children access and complete tasks and take ownership for their own learning, also supporting regular observations and assessments. Continue to work alongside Neil Farmer (EYFS consultant) to complete learning walks and identify areas for improvement Observe good practice in outstanding settings	**17th November** Learning walk with Neil Farmer (EYFS consultant) to see impact and decide on actions. **October** Lead and teachers to visit outstanding Reception setting, feedback to team and implement any changes to how we challenge the children.	Lead and teachers	17th Nov Wk of 19th Oct	Children will be suitably challenged based on their ability, which will show in the data of children making expected progress 76% of children will achieve GLD at the end of the year	Use 360 degree Appraisal system half termly, pupil progress meetings half termly
To close the gap between the achievement of Pupil Premium and non-Pupil Premium children.	Pupil progress meetings half termly to identify pupil premium children and their attainment to ensure they are working at age-related expectations Work with SENDco to identify targets and appropriate time-bonded interventions	**October and half termly** 360 degree learning walk to identify Pupil Premium children and look at provision for them	Lead and teachers	Half-termly meetings, Oct, Dec, Feb, May	Pupil Premium children who come in with low starting points will make accelerated progress	Pupil progress meetings, weekly planning sessions and head teacher drop-ins monthly

To develop more opportunities for moderation in nursery and pre-school to ensure data is accurate and allowing for specific time-bonded, effective interventions	Wednesday team meetings developed from start of term with all staff to meet in duos to update profiles, discuss the key children and create next steps to inform planning Look at structure of duo time meetings, ensuring it is an effective use of time. **October** Analyse data, do we have a stronger understanding of children's starting points to aid assessments as a result of duo times? If so, continue for next term.	Lead and teachers	Oct half term— see impact and continue if working	Children's data analysis and collection will be more rigorous, therefore next steps planning and provision will move learning on more quickly, resulting in 70% of all children leaving pre-school working at age-related expectations	Half-termly review meetings as a team to discuss the effectiveness of duo times and ways we can improve it once it is happening
To develop high engagement from parents to ensure they are actively involved in their child's learning	Links continued to be made with nursery/ pre-school and the children's centre to get parents more involved in their child's development, especially with Communication and language and reading 'Sing and story' events half termly across all of EYFS Develop times of termly parent consultations, depending on when the child starts and when a parent consultation is needed, to ensure summary sheets are used to report learning journey of child				
	October/November Develop & carry out 'sing and story' mornings and afternoons **Autumn term** Discuss with SLT when and how N/PS parent meetings should happen to have maximum impact on children's development	Lead and teachers	Continuous throughout the year	76% of children will achieve GLD at the end of Reception 80% of Pupil Premium children will achieve GLD at the end of Reception 70% of children will leave pre-school working at age-related expectations	Monitor the improvement in attendance of sing & story, parent consultations, children's centre classes, workshops. Use registers to monitor who is attending, to see if it's the same parents, and who we need to target

			Who	When	Success criteria	Monitoring
	Parent wall outside pre-school and nursery to continue constant communication of learning themes/key worker groups. Learning at home displays evident in each classroom using photos and quotes from parents. Monthly newsletters in pre-school and nursery. Workshops on 'how to play with children'. Nursery rhyme/story time challenge. Phonics, reading, maths learning meeting in Reception	**September** Develop learning at home, displays in classrooms. **Friday 25th September** Phonics workshop – introducing new sounds and recapping sounds we have learnt. **October** Set up workshops and story rhyme time challenges once children have settled. **Monthly** Telling parents dates, themes, reminders etc.				360 monitoring and case studies of children with SEND
Work alongside SENDco and other external agencies to ensure correct/ appropriate SEND provision is put in place, time-bonded and impact is measured to ensure children with SEND make appropriate progress	Regular half-termly meetings with health visitor to discuss key individuals. SENDco to be an integral part in pupil progress and attainment meetings to give support and guidance on provision for children with SEND	**Half-termly** PPA meetings, SenCo committed to spending half a day a week supporting SEND children and observing provision to give instant feedback on what more we can do	Lead and teachers	Half-termly, ongoing	Children with SEND will make the expected progress that is targeted for them.	

		Half-termly	Lead and teachers	Weekly with half-termly reviews to measure impact	Learning walks	Learning walks, drop-ins
To create systems to ensure the environment in maintained and always well-equipped and organised to support learning	Create systems to maintain the environment that are disseminated between staff members on a weekly rolling programme. Every staff member is responsible for that job and will be held to account by each other. Thursday after-school time to be set aside for changeover/display updating	Review to see how team feel about the roles and how we are managing them			will show that the environment in EYs is welcoming, tidy, well-organised and maximising opportunities for learning	
Close the gap between the attainment of boys and girls across EYFS (from last year's data, biggest gaps in Communication and Language and Literacy)	Continue to ensure staff understand the boy's interests in their key groups and plan accordingly to them. Develop Communication and Language opportunities that will engage boys using their interests as a stimulus for role play. Use learning detectives as a way to engage the boys in challenging themselves. Develop book corner to appeal to boys, using interest-led comics and magazines etc. to engage them. Work alongside Neil Farmer to get advice/ideas to implement good practice for supporting boys learning in EYFS	**Half-termly** Data analysis to see how boys are achieving compared to girls, review and adjust plans according to data	Lead and teachers	Every half term	Data will show that the gap between boys and girls attainment is closing	Half-termly data analysis looking at gender gaps and identifying specific areas to focus on

Bibliography and further reading

Britto, P. B. (2012), 'School Readiness: A Conceptual Framework'. UNICEF (www.unicef.org/education/files/Chil2Child_ConceptualFramework_FINAL(1).pdf)

Department for children, schools and families (2008), *Practice Guidance for the Early Years Foundation Stage*. Crown copyright

DfE (2015), *Early Years Foundation Stage Profile Results in England, 2015*. Crown copyright

DfE (2014), *Statutory Framework for the Early Years Foundation Stage: Setting the Standards for Learning, Development and Care for Children From Birth to Five*. Crown copyright

DfE (2013), *Early Years Outcomes: A Non-statutory Guide for Practitioners and Inspectors to Help Inform Understanding of Child Development Through the Early Years*. Crown copyright

Dweck, C. 2012), *Mindest: How You Can Fulfill Your Potential*. New York: Ballantine Books

Dweck, C. 'What does this mean for me?'. www.mindsetonline.com/whatisit/whatdoesthismeanforme

Early Education (2012), *Development Matters in the Early Years Foundation Stage (EYFS)*. Crown copyright

Foundation Years website: 'Fundamental British values in the Early Years' (www.foundationyears.org.uk/files/2015/03/Fundamental_British_Values.pdf)

Goddard Blythe, S. (2000), 'First steps to the most important ABC'. TES newspaper

Goddard Blythe, S. (2009), *Attention, Balance and Co-ordination - the A,B,C of Learning Success*. Wiley-Blackwell.

Kennedy, S. P. (2001), 'Freedom for speech: outdoor play and its potential for young children's conceptual, linguistic and communicative development'. EdD thesis, The Open University.

Kirklees Council (2013), 'Kirklees guidance for transitions in the Early Years'. Kirklees Council

Laevers, F. (ed) translated by Laevers, H. (2005), 'Well-being and involvement in care settings: a process-oriented self-evaluation instrument'. Kind & Gezin and the Research Centre for Experientel Education, Leuven University

(www.kindengezin.be/img/sics-ziko-manual.pdf)

Laevers, F. and Heylen, L. (eds) (2003) *Involvement of Children and Teacher Style: Insights From an International Study on Experiential Education*. Leuven University Press

Leithwood, K. A. and Riehl, C. (2003): 'What We Know about Successful. School Leadership', Report by Division A of AERA

Pascal, C and Bertram, T. (1999), 'The Effective Early Learning Project: The Quality of Adult Engagement in Early Childhood Settings in the UK'. University College Worcester, Centre for Research in Early Childhood Education

Ofsted (2015), *School Inspection Handbook*. Crown copyright

Ofsted (2015), *Early Years Inspection Handbook*. Crown copyright

Ofsted (2015), *Teaching and play in the early years – a balancing act?* Crown copyright

Sanders, L. (2014), 'A hungry brain slurps up a kid's energy'. Science News

Kuzawa, C. et al(2014), 'Metabolic costs and evolutionary implications of human brain development'. Proceedings of the National Academy of Sciences, August 25.

Saluja, G., Scott-Little, C. and Clifford, R. M. (2000), 'Readiness for school: a survey of state policies and definitions'. Early Childhood Research and Practice

Siraj I, Hallet E,(2014) *Effective and Caring Leadership in The Early Years*. London: Sage

Wong, M. and Csikszentmihalyi, M. (1991). 'Motivation and academic achievement: The effects of personality traits and the quality of experience'. Journal of Personality 59: 539–574.